Artists & Artisans

# ROUNDABOUT
# PEOPLE

*Front of speedway ride artwork by Mark Gill, at The Village, Fleggburgh, 1997*

Previous publications

*The Rodeo Switchback moves from Fovant to Hollycombe*, November 1993
*Jump On, Jump On*, ISBN 0 902830 33 3, October 1994
*UK Gallopers* on the Carousel website, from February 1996

# Artists & Artisans

# ROUNDABOUT PEOPLE

by

**Brian Steptoe**

JUMPER BOOKS

Published by Jumper Books
Wokingham, Berkshire, England

Text and photographs copyright © Brian Steptoe, 1998

ISBN 0 9523112 1 6

A CIP catalogue record for this book is available
from the British Library

Printed in England by BAS Printers, Over Wallop, Hampshire
on Fineblade Smooth paper

# Contents

# Acknowledgements

My gratitude is extended to all those who agreed to being interviewed during the preparation of this book and for the care they have given in their comments and suggested improvements. Thanks are also given to those who have allowed me to photograph their work or their rides and apologies are offered to those who, for reasons of cost and space, have had to be omitted from the final version.

I would like to extend many thanks for the meticulous feedback given at the draft layout stages by fair historians Paul Braithwaite and Stephen Smith. I hope they feel that the quality of the result has been worthwhile and reflects the time they have given to this project.

Thanks are also extended to my many friends in North America, who accepted my wife Jean and myself – *those two Brits* – as sharing their own interests in traditional carousels. The chapter outlining the very large subject of US carousels and their history in the short form here has been produced from material gathered at three National Carousel Association conventions. Gratitude is extended to all those whose equipment is illustrated and to those whose input at these conventions has allowed this section of the book to be written.

# Introduction

The artistic skills and artisan crafts that are involved behind the scenes in maintaining the attraction of the old time fairground roundabout, with its bright colours, lights and fair organ music, are an excellent example of work being carried out as much for love as for money.

The objective of this book is to celebrate the skills and fortitude of such 'roundabout people' in maintaining the best traditions from the past, keeping these alive at the end of the 1990s, when so much is done to prescriptions set by accounting rules. 'Roundabout People' are described here by examples selected from those who carve, paint or restore rides and those who operate them.

Whenever the subject of fairground art is raised it always gives rise to the question, 'But is it art?' Certainly it is *commercial* art and many of the carved animals and items or decor from earlier rides are very definitely collectable as antique objects. Recent proof of this was the successful auction of the Tussauds Collection of Fairground Art at Wookey Hole, Somerset, carried out by Christie's in October 1997.

The aims of fairground art and carving have always been commercial – to attract custom by appealing to everyday folk visiting the fairs. A useful discussion on the distinctions between what is termed 'people's art' and 'high art' is given in *People's Art*, by Emmanuel Cooper, published in 1994. He states that judgements about fairground art, amongst other similar styles, should be made by assessment of its fitness for the intended purpose and how creative the artist who has made it has been. This is in contrast to high art, where aesthetics, historical background and critical review are relevant factors.

This book builds on those aspects of my first fairground book, *Jump On, Jump On*, that dealt with the culture and stories of the people involved, but this time with more direct attention to the centrepiece of the traditional fair or carnival: the merry-go-round, the carousel, the 'gallopers'. There are just a few diversions here and there along the way to add variety.

Following the approach taken by several television documentary series, the aim has been to convey a lifestyle through a series of personal interviews – snapshots, with the roundabout theme as a thread running through, with different viewpoints from each of the people involved. What will be noticed is that in very many cases the artists and craftsmen described have been self-taught or taught by example. Formal artistic training almost never features in their learning process.

For practical reasons, this a selective rather than a comprehensive study and I am conscious of the many individuals who are involved with galloper rides who are not included. Duplication of my earlier book has been avoided as far as possible by choice of individuals not previously featured.

Links through marriage between travelling showfolk families are well known to members of that community and to historians and others interested in their culture. The stories that are unfolded in this book also show an element of linkage, in this instance not by family but rather through supplier and customer relationships, through friendships and through ownership links of some of the rides. Readers are invited to trace these as they read through the stories.

Many of the merry-go-rounds that still exist today were originally built and populated with craftsmen-carved and decorated animals over 100 years ago. This applies in all the developed countries around the world, in America and mainland Europe as well as in the United Kingdom. The rides that remain have become antiques, precious heirlooms, sometimes neglected or ignored, but still having a working role in the amusement industry. They are a tradition, for both young and old, an introduction to more thrill-laden and stomach-churning rides, a reminder of past times. In fact, along with similar gentle rides, they provide a true family-oriented source of entertainment. John Carter, who, with his family, operates a traditional old-time fair in and around London, remarks 'The imagination of a child at the age of seven or eight is a precious thing, something to be nurtured. My aim is to give these youngsters rides on which they can for a while fulfil the imaginings of their own world.'

In the past the pride of the owners of these major fairground rides found expression in many ways. As Jimmy Noyce, one such owner with his brother Tommy, says, 'In the old days every owner would have a photograph taken each season of their family alongside the ride. The senior member would command all to attend, even if there might have been internal family quarrels as obstacles on other occasions.' Showmen had a true pride in what they presented and tradition was everything.

About half of the remaining galloper rides in the UK are still travelling, sometimes regularly, sometimes less so. They do not have the advantage of 'friends' groups of volunteers to help with preservation and restoration, a process that has been encouraged to take place particularly in North America, where permanent carousels in local amusement parks operating through the seasons have created a stronger link with local inhabitants.

Successfully operating these rides year-in and year-out demands investment of time, money and effort. Standards of safety have to be maintained and improved. Standards of quality need similar attention: carving, decoration, lighting, operating smoothness and accompanying music all have a part to play. These original rides were built in times when wages were low and staff were very much more readily available. The effort to travel and operate these labour intensive rides is considerable and today 'I'm knackered, absolutely knackered' is a terse remark often heard at the end of the travelling season, as the weather deteriorates and winter approaches.

Many of the people presenting these rides nowadays are doing it as a hobby rather than as a business, Keen preservationists and operators, perhaps just aiming to cover their costs, as well as long-established travelling showmen and their families seeking to earn a living, form the complex and sometimes politically contrary mix who provide the offerings available to the public, to the punters. Let us have a look behind the scenes at some of the people and skills involved.

TRADITIONS FROM THE PAST

# Traditions from the past

*'For up an' down an' round, said 'e, goes all appointed things, an' losses on the roundabouts means profits on the swings'*, P.R.Chalmers, *Green Days & Blue Days* (1912).

The relative status of and interest in fairground roundabouts rises and falls almost as fast as the galloping mounts themselves. In the 1960s a low was reached when many owners sold their wooden animals to the antique trade. In the mid-1990s it seemed as if these rides were coming back into favour with the public and several new and restored sets appeared at major fairs and steam rallies. Only a few years later three or four sets of gallopers have been put up for sale, their owners perhaps disillusioned by the money-taking ability of their ride. For sure, a ride has to be very attractively presented to have a chance of earning a reasonable share of the change in people's pockets, requiring ongoing expenditure by the owner.

Gallopers in England may all look the same to the casual visitor. In fact there are genuine old machines (equivalent to the US 'antique' carousels), reproduction sets including some early-dated components and rides of recent manufacture. Some of the best examples of old sets include those now travelled by John Forrest, Jimmy & Tommy Noyce, Carters Steam Fair, Jack & Judith Schofield and Bobby Rawlins. Then there are the Pettigroves who travel the only set of gallopers that has been owned by the same family since it was new in the 1880s. This family have sometimes suffered setbacks, most recently when Michael Bacon, who had been operating and working on restoring the ride, was killed in a road accident outside their winter quarters in 1995.

In the UK today there is a complete mixture of galloper owners. Many sets are still the property of long established fairground travelling showmen. These are members of the Showmen's Guild and have rights to present their rides at established fairs whose history may go back hundreds of years. 'King John gave me the right to build my equipment up here' is a quoted claim if long-established traditions are challenged.

There are more recent owners, attracted to the way of life, operating as independent showmen who see a traditional set of gallopers as synonymous with the lifestyle. Best described as entrepreneurs, they are responsible for establishing their own places to appear and reliant on their fairground equipment for a living. Then there are those attracted through the preservation route, seeing the renovation or rebuild of a set of gallopers more as a hobby interest with a money-earning aspect. All shades within this spectrum of classification and motivation exist in practice.

### Amusement Parks

The artistry featured in this book is centered on the travelling fair business, which was the source for many of the skills involved. Most of these are equally relevant to the fixed amusement park industry. Blackpool Pleasure Beach, one of the UK's best known amusement parks, opened in 1896 and was preceded by an American Long-built carousel installed on the beach in 1895. It shared the south shore with fortune tellers and others from the gypsy encampment which was there at that time. Trimpers Amusement Park in Maryland USA is included in the chapter on the American scene. This park predates the Blackpool Pleasure Beach by three years. A number of English seaside piers and parks have very early origins, Blackgang Chine on the Isle of Wight, which opened in 1842 being listed as the third earliest in the world (information from the National Amusement Parks Historical Association).

### Shottesbrooke Great Steam Fair

The watershed which re-established old-time fairground rides as viable 'modern' attractions for the public was the 1964 Great Steam Fair at Shottesbrooke Park in Berkshire. There was a similar event put together at Stratford-upon-Avon that year, but with more limited success. The one-off Shottesbrooke Fair was organised by John Smith, now Sir John Smith and firmly holds its place in UK fairground history. It might be likened to the formation of what became the National Carousel Association in the USA and the publication of Fred Fried's book on the history of carousels in that very same year of 1964. Noyce's gallopers and Cole's Aspland switchback were there, chosen to represent the old-time merry-go-round rides. Noyces still travel their ride and the switchback now operates at the Thursford Collection in Norfolk. Readers will read more about the Great Steam Fair in following chapters.

## Losses and Rescues

No book on 'roundabout people' would be complete without mention of the antique and collector trade. It is a part of the history that many may wish had not happened, but as well as the upheavals it caused it nonetheless raised recognition and awareness of values associated with fairground memorabilia, much of which was unused and slowly decaying in showmen's yards across the country. Many galloper owners were attracted by the interest in roundabout animals which arose in the 1960s and early 1970s. Rides which were either already unused or seen as poor money-earners were stripped of their horses. Replacements in glass fibre were made or all too often all that remained of the ride was scrapped. Today many of the old rides that remain are populated with a mix of glass fibre and wooden animals.

Relic Designs of London ran annual auctions of fairground animals and other artefacts up until 1996. These events were the only specialist sales of fairground items in Britain and were jointly organised with Eddy and Marjory Bangor from 1977. Lord and Lady Bangor ran an antique shop called *Trad* in Portobello Road, London from 1962 which operated until the mid 1980s. Marjory, who died in 1990, established her own collection of fairground items, which was housed at Wookey Hole in Somerset until auctioned off in the autumn of 1997.

Some galloper owners feel strongly that animals on a ride must be wood rather than glass fibre to properly reflect the historic origins of these ubiquitous rides. When Colin Jones rescued the remains of a stripped ride from the USA around 1990, he had a full set of new animals carved for the ride. James Graham, who has restored an 1885 'dobby' set that the family bought in 1984 using glass fibre horses, has had the outside row of twelve horses carved in wood for use on the ride on special occasions.

roundabouts, Tim Waterstone has introduced rides complete with ten carved wood animals at the first of his new chain of stores for children's goods, commencing in 1997.

*fig 1*
*Anderson-carved horse being stripped and repainted by Bill Potter at the Bressingham Steam Collection, Norfolk*

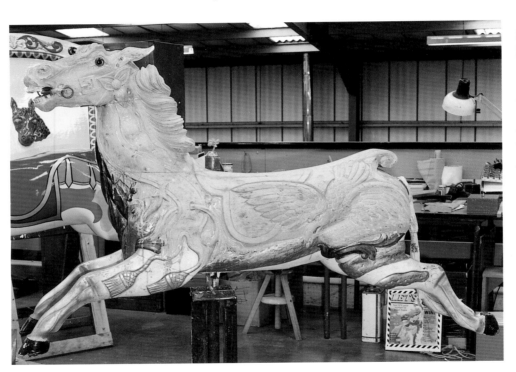

### Makers, Carvers and Painters

The original manufacturers of English gallopers and earlier versions without the up and down galloping action, called 'dobby' sets, are summarised here. Readers seeking greater detail are referred to other books on the topic, such as *Fairground Art* by Weedon and Ward. Broadly the dates involved range from the 1880s until the 1920s. A short list to act as a reminder here would include Savage of Kings Lynn, the largest volume makers, Tidman of Norwich and Walker from Tewkesbury. Each of these employed or

The Bradley family from Lancashire acquired the remains of some old sets of gallopers in 1997 and are intent upon restoring a ride with wooden rather than glass fibre mounts.

In the more modest arena of juvenile

*fig 2*
*New three-abreast*
*gallopers built by*
*Rundle Engineering,*
*with paintwork by*
*Bobby Ayers, installed*
*in 1996 at the Palace*
*Pier, Brighton, Sussex*

contracted carvers for the animals and the ride decoration. The most well-known carvers were the Anderson family of Bristol who originally carved ships figureheads, shop signs and work for churches. J.R. Anderson joined his uncle in the business in 1865 and from the 1880s he turned his hand to carving fairground animals. After 1913, his son A.E. Anderson took over and continued to carve these until his death in 1936. Another major firm were Orton, who later merged to become Orton & Spooner, from Burton-on-Trent. They produced very elaborate carving, including animals and also made a range of fairground rides, living wagons and stalls, notably elaborate scenic and switchback rides.

The most well-known fairground painters were Edwin Hall and Fred Fowle, who joined forces and worked together in London until the 1960s. Numerous painters were trained in the Hall & Fowle paintshop and many others have developed these skills within the travelling fairground community. The brighter colours introduced by Fred Fowle set the style for many of the traditional fairground painters of today. Mark Gill is one such artist and an example of his work is shown as the frontispiece in this book. Another recent artist whose skills are particularly sought after for 'antiquing' fairground animals is Katie Morgan.

The older subdued fairground colours used for example by Orton & Spooner were replaced by bright primary colours from the late 1930s, when both Hall and Fowle worked for the ride manufacturers Lakins in London. Fred Fowle took a lead in this after World War Two and his styles were much imitated right through until airbrush based painting came to the fore on modern rides in the 1980s. An interview with Fred Fowle when he was 63 was included in the catalogue of the 1977 fairground art exhibition held at the Whitechapel Gallery, London, written by Ian Starsmore.

Newly manufactured sets of gallopers are commissioned from time to time, both for amusement park sites and for travelling. In the winter of 1993/4 the Bishton showman family constructed what was reported in the *World's Fair* trade newspaper as the first new three-abreast set built in the UK for about 60 years. J.H.Rundle and Company completed a new four-abreast set in 1995 which is at Loudoun Castle in Scotland and a three-abreast set for the Noble Organisation which was installed on Brighton Palace Pier in 1996. The Mardi Gras (UK) Ltd company have also built several new machines since 1995, including one for travelling showman Albert Botton which made its first appearance in 1997.

# Fairground Painters

## John Hatwell

Johnny Hatwell is a well-known fairground painter and gilder. He is from an established family of Oxfordshire showmen who lived originally at Cassington, north of Oxford. Like many showmen, he can turn his hand to several crafts, but regards painting in the old traditional styles as his first love. He lost his wife Sue in September 1995. He has two sons, Bradley and Gregory and lives at Carterton in Oxfordshire.

### Johnny's education

Johnny used to go to school when his family came back to Cassington after each travelling season. He attended until he was about twelve, but being away for much of the year he missed out on much of his schooling. He can read and write but is not so good at spelling. Of course he regrets it now. Frequently there were things he had to ask Sue about or have her look up in a dictionary. Like all travelling fairground families, his *real* education had to include learning from the family and on the fairground.

When Johnny was at school his school-teacher was rather more interested in him doing art than learning to spell. He remembers her saying 'Put your hand up if anyone wants to

*fig 3*
*Johnny Hatwell with a typical example of his scrollwork, at his workshop in Carterton*

draw something on this blackboard.' Perhaps being more used to standing up in front of people, young Johnny went to the front of the class and was handed the chalk. The teacher and all the class were looking at him, because none of the other children wanted to go up there. She would be thinking that Johnny was going to draw some leaves or something like that but John had seen his uncle doing fairground decoration and so he would draw out fleur-de-lis type scroll work. His teacher would be tickled pink and would say 'John, what does it represent?' 'Well miss, what it represents is the fairground scroll work what goes on swinging boats.' And so he would then have to talk to the class about travelling with the fair.

John also remembers the schoolteacher taking the class on nature walks in the spring. All the primroses would be out and the children would take a leaf and go back to the class where they had to draw it. He started to do this and found that he was very good at it.

John's father was George Hatwell, who was the carpenter in the family, whilst his uncle 'Buller' Hatwell was the engineer and Uncle Jack was the painter. Uncle Jack was considered an excellent craftsman for carrying out scrolling, lettering and lining, working down in the family barn at Cassington.

One clear early memory of John's was when the family used to go and buy their brushes in Birmingham. He went with them to a big old-fashioned shop at the Fiveways junction. Where other children might be looking at Hornby train sets, Johnny remembers preferring to look in the glass cases at all the lining brushes and sables and the writing brushes and the quills. A lining brush then would cost about two shillings, in pre-decimal money. His father would buy John a few brushes so that he could start his fairground 'learning' by painting a pair of steps. He would paint the steps in maroon and line them all out as well. He was not very good at it at the start, but that was how he started out, learning as he painted. After a while, showmen would ask, 'John, can you paint some number plates on my lorry?' They used to give him about five shillings for it.

The showmen in those days would do painting on the fairground before they built up, something that John disapproves of nowadays.

The first thing he remembers painting for a

showman outside his own family was a large autodrome. He was about fifteen at the time. The ride needed to be smartened up for a film job, '*Saturday Night and Sunday Morning*', starring Albert Finney. Filming of the autodrome was done on the fairground at Southall. His artwork was based on the art deco flying Mercury wing designs which were very popular at that time.

## The Hatwell's juvenile roundabout

John Hatwell is well-known nowadays for travelling the family's juvenile roundabout. It is a Lakin machine, built in about 1928. The first owner was a Yorkshire showman who was unable to keep up payment instalments on it. In those days the owners would put the bailiffs in and fetch the machines back. John's father found it in a yard in London. He had difficulty himself in those hard times in finding the money for it, but John thinks he paid about forty-five pounds, in the early 1930's.

All the scenery that was originally on the roundabout was Dutch scenes of windmills and dykes painted by Edwin Hall, which would be worth a lot of money today. John's father didn't think the Dutch scenes were very attractive and

he had them painted over. That Lakin ride could be supplied to build up either as a 'swing-out' set or with platforms. Hatwell's one had two big carved whales with it, like those on the big scenic rides in the early 1900s. They could put the whales on together with peacocks and horses with twisted rods, or they could build up with the platforms. There were biplanes and pedal cars with petrol cans on their running boards that fitted on the platforms. These were all Triang-made toys, which would be worth a considerable sum today.

The seats in the whales were all plush, but the children would not ride in them because of the creature's teeth. His father had put a red lamp in their mouths and the kids used to be frightened of them. They would go on the peacocks and the horses but not on those whales. John remembers his dad selling the six peacocks and the two whales. Later, the platform toys were just thrown away, down on the local dump. Many showmen dumped things that would be worth a fortune today. John himself remembers selling a Clayton & Shuttleworth showman's traction engine for five pounds.

He remembers minding the ride once when

he was a young boy at Oxford St Giles fair and a man came up in a Crombie overcoat and a black Homberg hat. John's father said to his son

*fig 4*
*The Hatwell's Lakin-built juvenile roundabout*

'John, I want you to meet this gentleman. This is Mr Lakin, Bob Lakin. He wants to buy the roundabout back.' But his father wouldn't sell it.

### John's painting work

'I'll paint anything, modern or whatever, but I really love doing old-fashioned lettering and scrolling. I get carried away. When I'm doing a job like that for anyone, I'm really doing it for myself as well as for them.' He never uses the same style design twice. 'What I believe you've got to do is create it in your own head your own way. Otherwise people are going to say "look, that's Fred Fowle work" or whatever.'

One job he particularly remembers is when he repainted a juvenile roundabout which belonged to Lily Brewer. It was a Halstead made roundabout with German horses, Walker of Tewkesbury rounding boards and two vintage French-style Renault cars. Lily used to visit every week to see how John was getting on. John thinks she would have had a heart attack if she had come when he was burning the old paint off the rounding boards – there was a lot of carving on them! He considers that ride has the best horses of any juvenile roundabout he has seen.

John says that you have to judge lining out work by looking at where the lines turn. The lines should finish right at a sharp point without any overlaps. It shows bad '*education*' for a painter if there are overlaps.

## Some bad moments with gilding

John Hatwell remembers some tricky moments with his gilding. The gold size that is used to stick the leaf

*fig 5*
*John Hatwell busy lining out a top centre for David Downs gallopers*

to the work can go off very quickly and it is a mistake to try to do too much at a time. About eight years ago he worked on a vintage roundabout for Ken Anthony, a preservationist. All the lettering was in the old fairground style and all in gold leaf. It took hours and hours. Soon after it was collected John happened to be out, and

when he came back at night, there was this rounding board standing out by his shed. He said to Sue 'What's that roundabout board doing out there? Have they knocked it about taking it back?' Sue answered 'You spelt Generation wrong'. John had left the 'i' out!

Some other problem jobs stick in his mind. He has restored cockerels from church spires and there is not the opportunity to look at the job beforehand at close quarters. This particular one nearly led to him and his wife getting divorced! 'She had to throw my Sunday dinner out over it, and I love my Sunday roast. I was putting all this gold leaf on and I'd got down to the cockerel's neck and the size was going off. That bird was about five feet long and all black steel and there were little pit holes all over it. I wasn't very happy about that job. Even now I won't go to the village where the church is to look at it.'

John really loves working on traditional fairground art designs. As he says 'I watched the old painters doing their work and that's where I've got the knowledge. All those bright colours and shapes. On the transport as well as the rides. When you go on a fairground now, it's all drab, all browns and no gold.'

## Organ fronts

Five years ago Andrew Whitehead built John an organ. It came in a plain square cabinet and John made all the carved front himself. He had started doing some small carving work for showmen and preservationists who used to bring him horses for repainting. They would ask him to replace a missing ear or repair a broken leg. When Andrew rang up about the organ front, John said he would have a go at carving it himself. The first thing he started with was the fleur-de-lis on the top. His wife said 'I reckon you could do it all John.' He worked on the rest of it using a picture of a Chiappa organ as a reference and adding more detail on the baritone box at the front. John had the organ covered over when Andrew Whitehead came and he looked at his face as he took the cover off. 'John, I've to take my hat off to you', Andrew said, 'I didn't think it was going to look like this.'

Andrew said he would arrange for John to have some organ front work and within a week the phone went. The message was 'What about a proscenium for a German Ruth organ?' Knowing what this might entail John started to tremble, because he had only done the one organ and Andrew was talking about a German organ carved in the Black Forest. He would have to match his new carving with what was already there. When the job came, it was all beautiful carved flowers and buds. Swallowing hard and saying a little prayer to the *Man Above*, John got out his tape and measured along the bottom where the glockenspiel had to go. He drew out a design for the scroll and the new buds to match the carving already on the top. There were two layers of wood to carve to achieve the depth needed. But when he saw the finished organ playing at a Steam Rally at Fairford John remembers standing in front of it and feeling very pleased with his work. John believes that organ fronts have to be in the right style for the type of organ, Marenghi-style and Limonaire-style and so on. Some people going to rallies look at details like that to see if they are right for the particular make of organ.

## Varnishing techniques

John warms his varnish on a stove before 'flowing' it onto the work with a proper Hambleton round varnish brush. The varnished piece is left until the next day. 'You've got to get the temperature right in here and I can varnish five or six horses or centre boards together, as long as it's a good varnish.' He uses high-build yacht varnish which he puts on his stove, not right in the middle but a little away from the fire, just to warm it a little. 'What you've got to do, you lay it on, you don't try to spread it out. A lot of them say, "How do you get that glassy look, John?" You mustn't stand it up you see – it's got to lay down flat. If I do a set of rounding boards, I mustn't get standing them up. I don't shift anything which might make a dust for at least three days, to let the varnish harden. Varnish is funny stuff. If you see it when it's crinkley, someone has either varnished work in the sun, or over-varnished it when it's been too cold. You've got to get the temperature just right.'

But it is the painting that is really in John's blood. He would like his son Bradley to have this skill after him. 'I've had him in my work-shop here and said "just fill that bit in over there", you know. He'll have a go at it, but there's an art… This painting work, you either love it or you hate it.'

## David Downs Galloper work

John was working on David Downs galloper centres and some of his horses during early 1996. With the centre shutters, John picks up a chalk and a piece of hardboard and just looks and thinks what to put on them. As the design comes he is already thinking what the colours will be. 'All these mauves and that I mix myself.' John draws or cuts out his scroll designs and then turns the patterns over to give left or right

*fig 6*
*David Downs horses*
*painted by Johnny*
*Hatwell*

hand sides. The main thing is to ensure that the measurements are just right to fit in and leave suitable gaps.

Some jobs prove to be much more tricky that others. 'I've had some terrible jobs. Some-times when Sue used to come and fetch my tea into the shed, she'd say "You've been in here all day and how many of these boards have you done." "Well, I've just finally got the pattern laid out to fit the first one", I'd say.'

*fig 7*
*Dragon chariot side*
*for Wareham's*
*gallopers, painted by*
*Johnny Hatwell*

John has felt the loss of Sue very badly over the last two winters. It took a long while before he could start his painting work again. Eventually he brought himself to do it, coming into his shed in the morning, lighting the fire and playing an organ cassette tape to get into the right mood.

Whilst working on the final lining out on the shutters John said, 'Do you notice I'm not putting the lining brush on the end of where I stopped with the last stroke. I overlap the previous line and pull it out longer.' His father used to say just use matt paint for the lining. He would say 'Give it a coat of varnish after, my son.' With matt you can go much further with each brush stroke. But John prefers to work with gloss.

When customers come into John Hatwell's shed they see all his painting brushes sticking up in bean tins and they probably think 'This fellow, he's supposed to be a good painter, but those brushes in those tins don't look a lot'. But then John opens up his favourite box of brushes and shows them all his treasured sables. 'That one there, one of the best liners, that's called a *large swan*. Say if I was lining out a box truck, putting the edging round it, this is a nice brush for that. The brush names go by the birds.

There's a swan, a crow and a lark and so on.' Modern lining brushes come with long handles but Johnny Hatwell cuts most of the handle off, just leaving a little bit of wood. When he goes out he always take his brushes. 'I never leave them in this shed – they're *personal* to me.'

When he goes round the rally fields John looks at all the living vans and the lining out on them. Some are all right, but some of them, well...! 'We call 'em wagons – the flatties always say caravan.' Sometimes when he goes to a rally John sees an organ front that he has carved and decorated. 'I'm getting a bit big-headed now. I stand in front and the owner keeps on saying to anyone that comes up, "That's the gentlemen that done it." Johnny Hatwell can take a lot of that!

# Neddy Matthews

Neddy Matthews believes he has painted over 200 galloper horses, all in the old lorry that acts as his workshop. It dates from 1950 and was used for travelling his fairground stalls until it started to want money spent on it. Inside it measures just twenty one feet by seven feet six inches. Like many showmen, he has been involved with helping with film work and when some television people came to see him they could not understand how he could paint in this small space. He said, 'You've got to understand, we're *showmen*', as if that explains everything. He can work on six galloper horses at a time in that lorry, two set up on their hind legs and the other four on tables across its width, although he has to crawl under some of the horses to reach the full six. That is where his typical Matthews short, stocky build comes in useful.

Neddy Matthews was born in 1920 and his age is starting to catch up with him now. His driving days are over, as the law says his eyes are not good enough to drive on the road. 'Well, I can still shunt a truck in and that, but they've stopped me from driving because I'm diabetic and it's affected my eyes.' So he has had to hang up his driving license. It was still a clean one, even after sixty four years.

He is grateful that he can still do his painting. He loves painting and has done so as far back as he can remember as a child. He believes he was fortunate in growing up in the age when there were many skilled showmen about, those who really knew their job and who would help one of their own to acquire their skills and knowledge. They would not come along like they often do today, ready to just criticise. Ned remembers some of the names, 'Old Mr Wall, father of Buck Wall was a good man for scroll-work. Another was 'Tush' Stokes – the Stokes had gallopers. I'm talking about all galloper people, back in the 1930s.' Neddy was in his early teens then and he would soak up their experience like a sponge, talking about it for hours. They would be showing and telling him how to get things just right. As Ned reflects, 'I was stealing their brains and I was fortunate enough to have some good ones round me at the right time.'

### The Matthews family

Neddy lost both his parents when still young. His father died when he was eight years old and his mother when he was eighteen. He was fortunate in having good brothers and sisters, as there were three boys and six girls in the family and they were all close. Now only Neddy and his 83 year-old sister are still alive. Being a close family is wonderful but it comes very hard when you lose them. His mother was an invalid in a wheelchair for ten years, but the family soldiered on. 'She may have been in a chair, but she was still the guv'nor!'

Neddy was the baby of the family, the youngest grandson of William Matthews, who was born in 1843 in a showman's living van at Godalming in Surrey. He became known as 'Redshirt' because of dressing in that colour when he helped his father with the family's horse-turned roundabout. He bought a two-abreast steam-driven roundabout from Savages in 1883, which was pulled from fair to fair by horses, before the family had a steam engine.

Redshirt's story is told in Frances Brown's book *Fairfield Folk*.

Showmen say to Neddy 'You're a proper old Matthews, with your small size and your weight and that.' Neddy thinks with some pride, if they want to know anything about gallopers they always come over and ask *him*.

The Matthews family would travel round Surrey and Hampshire when his father and grandfather were alive. Most of the fairs in those days were just run by a single family, without other tenants on the ground. The family would travel with their gallopers, swingboats, a shooter and a coconut sheet. The sons and daughters would have their own stalls. He remembers when it was three balls for just tuppence on a coconut sheet and he has even seen gallopers riding for a halfpenny! One year a family he knows were letting children on their gallopers just in exchange for a jam jar. The children used to bring the jam jars and they would let them have a ride. Then the next day the showmen would take the jars up to the totters yard to sell them. Recycling was going on even then!

As a youngster Neddy remembers going round the grounds and picking things up to earn a few coppers. 'When I was a child they used to have what they called a squirter table. A squirter was like a toothpaste tube full of water. Then there was confetti that the kids threw at one another and the boys put down the girl's backs. We'd go round the ground and pick up all the empty tubes, take them all back and get ourselves sixpence. We were well made with that.'

He remembers what he recalls as the golden days of his youth, even though some people would call them the hard days. The Matthews used to open at Reading fair and travel to places like Ripley, Alton, Petersfield, Cranleigh and Chiddingfold, towns and villages in Surrey and Hampshire. He considers that all the travelling showmen took pride in what they were doing in those days. Many had steam engines then, and Neddy says that the decoration on the engines and later the lorries, to keep them spic and span, are what made him take up painting.

*fig 8*
*Neddy Matthews in his ball joint*

He can remember the first time he was ever in charge of a horse, when he was about ten. Some of the men had left the fair and everyone in the family had to pitch in and help. His sisters had to steer the engines and Neddy, the youngest in the family, was to drive the horse. Such excitement – 'I was going to be in charge of a horse! No one sitting on it with me.' As it turned out, the horse knew all the routine. All Neddy did was hold the reins and when the steam engines started or stopped, so the horse started and stopped as well.

A little later on, when he was around twelve, Neddy became the stoker on an engine. That involved putting the injectors on for the water and making the fire up. He had a crafty little drive himself when the opportunity arose. He was taught how to steer by driving the steam engine round and round the fair field. He has been right through the various forms of transport, 'I've driven horses, steam engines, solid tyre lorries, and the modern lorries, right up to the present day. Now I've got a motor out there that's only three years old and I'm not allowed to drive it! Seventy seven years it took to get myself a good motor and now it's just a monument.'

## A little learning, but not a lot

Neddy recognises that he is no scholar in the three R's meaning of the word. He had very little schooling and the few times he did attend, they were not interested in a showman's child at all. 'They took you because the law said you had to go to school. You sat in a corner with a bit of paper and a pen and that was that. You were not even part of the class in those days.'

He reckons he learnt more when he was in the army in World War Two. One night they said he was to be on telephone orderly duty. Neddy said to the sergeant, 'I can't do that sergeant, 'cos I can't read nor write, I'm no scholar.' The sergeant said 'I've heard all the excuses in the world, but that's a new one on me. But you'll do it! Get in there and do it or you'll find yourself on a charge.' So there he was that night, praying for the telephone not to ring. Of course it did. He had to take down the message as best he could. What he could not spell, he drew. The next morning he was having breakfast when he hears – 'Matthews, get over to the orderly room and don't let your feet touch the ground.' When he arrived the officer said 'Matthews, are there any messages or have you just used this for doodling on.' 'No sir,' said Neddy, 'the messages are all there', and he interpreted what he had drawn and read them out. He had just done the best he could, like anyone worth their salt as a showman has to do. Neddy was sent to the Army School of Education where they told him he was word-blind. He could just read a few letters and then his mind would cut out. As he says, 'I'm may be illiterate, but I'm not ignorant.'

Showmen said to Neddy when he came out

of the army 'You're a showman, a fairground showman. Tell me how you had six years in the army and came out with a clean sheet.' Neddy's answer was 'There's a very thin red line and I toed it, but never did step over it, even if my toe-cap might have just nudged it sometimes. When I got called up the sergeant major told us "We don't punish you for what you do, we punish you for getting caught doing it". So I never got caught.'

## Galloper work

Neddy Matthews recalls the many sets of gallopers he has painted in his workshop. 'There was a set for Rose that used to be in Chessington Zoo, a set for Marshall Hill which was down on Hayling Island and the Noyce's gallopers when they first had them. At that time they were in a worse state than those that Jimmy Graham had when his first came from Wilmot's. They were in a deplorable state, just about workable but on their last legs.' Neddy, his brother Joe, Mr Noyce senior and a couple of friends worked all one summer and winter on that set. When they started, none of the horses would gallop and there were just six straight battens of lights left on the ride. Neddy reckons his sidestall has more light on it than those gallopers had at the start. Now it is thought of as one of the best sets in the country.

When it came to the set belonging to Jimmy Graham from Scotland, Jimmy said that he would like to get the horses painted up. 'The only ones I like are your ones' said Jimmy. 'I've seen a lot of other horses painted up, but my father (his father was alive at the time) said, "Looking at the horses on Noyce's gallopers at Nottingham fair, that's how I want ours done".' 'Wait a minute' Neddy said, 'before you start, I'm not a professional, I'm only a showman that can do a bit of painting. Whether it's good enough for you or not ...' Jimmy replied 'From what I've seen on Noyce's, it would suit me'. When Neddy mentioned that Scotland was a long way from his workshop, Jimmy confirmed that he would bring the work to Neddy and take it back again when completed. Neddy felt that there must be a painter in the 500 miles between where he worked and Scotland. Jimmy insisted '*No*, you've got what I want and I don't care how far I've got to come to get it'. That was a great compliment and they ended up as very good friends. Neddy has painted all the horses for him, both glass fibre and wooden ones.

James Horton, who used to go and help the Noyce's on their machine was really *bitten* by gallopers. He would travel miles to help them, even up to Nottingham Goose Fair. When he

Neddy thinks of himself as a traditional fairground style of painter, which is what he really enjoys, although he will do any style of fairground painting that people want. 'But it's the traditional work that people mostly come to me for.'

*fig 9*
*Bottom shutter of*
*'Jolly Tubes' painted*
*by Neddy Matthews*

was about eighteen years old James said to Neddy 'I'm going to have a set of gallopers one day.' Later, after he bought the parts for a set of from Jack Schofield, James came round to see Neddy. 'Well look James,' Neddy said 'If you want to start on your horses, bring some round.' So James had the horses and the droppers painted. Some nights they would be painting until two o'clock in the morning to get the work done. Neddy really gives him credit for the effort he put into his gallopers.

## Neddy's animals

Neddy still goes out travelling, with his daughter and son-in-law. He does some painting in the summer on the grounds for showmen. His daughter is married to Johnny Coneley's son and they travel a set of dodgems and a round-up. Neddy goes with them during the summer, travelling with a living van and his stall. Neddy's two dogs go with him. One is 'Cagney', a German Shepherd and the other is 'Wolf', a Belgian Shepherd. Anyone visiting Neddy is certain to

*fig 10*
*Galloper horse for James Horton. The horses were painted by Neddy Matthews and James*

remember his dogs, because as Ned says, really they're *too* protective.

In the past he kept pet rabbits as well. People would call in to see him when he was painting and there would be rabbits running about loose in his workshop or in summer running about in his 'joint'. The only time they went in their box was at night. Mr Coneley remembers that when Neddy had his rabbits, in the evening there would be a 'thump, thump, thump' in his lorry. Ned would say 'I haven't said goodnight to the rabbits yet'. They would not settle down until he went up and cuddled them and said, 'Goodnight mate'.

Neddy loves animals. He remembers being at a 'paid-do' at Olympia with his coconut sheet. The Chipperfield circus family were there with lions and tigers. The event was really a glorified drink-up and everyone had a good night. The beer flowed to the point where it was being poured down the helter-skelter there like a waterfall. Chipperfields had their lions cage built up but their men had done a moonlight flit. Johnny Coneley was there as well and he said to Neddy, 'They'll be short of men.' So they went over to help. Johnny said, 'Give him a hand to put the stands up in that cage.' So Ned was in the cage and all of a sudden one tiger went past him, followed by another. He could not put those stands up quick enough. As Neddy says, 'It's the nearest point I've been to diarrhoea without it happening.' When Chipperfield thanked Neddy for helping and found out who he was, he said 'Matthews, what Matthews are you?, Was your mother a Chittock?' When Neddy said 'Yes.' he replied, 'No wonder you could go in there with them! It's born in you' (Chittocks were an old circus family). Neddy answered, 'I hope that the tigers knew. It may have been born in me but I thought it was coming out!'

## It's a gift

Neddy has some brushes in his workshop that are around fifty years old. Some belonged to 'Tush' Stokes and others belonged to a showman named Arnold from the Isle of Wight. As Neddy says, 'A good brush gives me a good reputation. If a scroll goes wrong, it's down to me and not the brush I'm using. When painting scrolls I say "Someone up there is guiding me".

A man once said to him 'What do you use as a colour chart? Where do you get the colours from?' Neddy's reply was, 'Out there. The gold corn, the blue sky, the green and the brown from the leaves on the trees and the sunset. All those colours you can capture. If you can capture those into the work you're doing, you're going to give someone the beauty that you see yourself.' As Neddy says, it is a gift. He certainly has not gained his skill from books, but from life and from friends and teachers on the fairgrounds.

# John Pockett

Ever since he can ever remember, John Pockett has had a great love all the three travelling people – gypsies, fairground showmen and circus folk. His annual Christmas treat was to go to Bertram Mills Circus at Olympia in London. He is interested in anything where there is a moveable dwelling involved which could be here today and gone tomorrow.

Much of John's childhood was spent in the Sutton and Cheam area of Surrey during the early 1950s. He remembers the fair at Cheam, a very simple one built up in the street. There would just be a set of gallopers, some swing-boats, a juvenile or two and a few hoopla stalls. John always thought it was the most wonderful thing – it came one day and went the next. All the showmen's living vans were the old traditional ones and these would be parked in the road where he lived. The gallopers belonged to Bert Searle and they could *just* be built up in the middle of the road. There was an organ in the ride and all the locals would complain about the dreadful, appalling noise it made.

Other fairs that attracted him as a youngster included those at Mitcham and at Epsom Downs. He thought Mitcham was a fabulous fair and even his mother remembered great days in *her* childhood there. The Derby fair at Epsom Downs was also of special interest because both the gypsies and the fairground people were there at the same time. This mix of interests is unusual, because people that are interested in the showmen often don't have any interest in gypsies and vice versa.

## Wartime evacuation

John was born in 1942 and when he was very young, his mother was evacuated down to Somerset, where they lived with the family in a farmworker's cottage. He recalls that much of the farm work then was still carried out using horses. The cottage was at the top of a dead-end lane where it joined a road to the nearest village. Halfway down this lane there were some very poor gypsies living in vans and there was also an encampment of gypsies where the lane came to a dead end at the bottom. There were a brother and sister living in that encampment. Their mother had died and although they had not burnt

*fig 11*
*John Pockett with a*
*horse from his*
*juvenile roundabout*

her wagon in true Romany tradition, it was shut up and never ever used again. They were named Jowles. They used to come up for water to the farmworkers cottage where John's mother was

living. The brother Jowles used to dress in old-fashioned clothes – breeches and shoes with buckles. He would ride around on a white horse and everyone was frightened of him. Wherever John's mother went walking with John in his pram, this gypsy would be looking at her over the hedge from his horse. John cannot remember any of that himself but one thing he *can* remember is being looked at by a group of gypsy children when he was in his pram. 'All these little raggedy-taggedy dark faces.' Perhaps these were the foundations of his later interest.

**First working days**

When John left school, he thought he would like the open air life and started out by working on farms in the Surrey and Sussex area. He would live in the farmhouse with the farmer's family. At that time any gypsies that there were about would still use horse-drawn wagons. Once again he found there were some of them camping at the top of the road where he lived.

John was so drawn to the travelling life that in 1959 he bought a gypsy caravan to restore and live in. It was a simple straight-sided wagon, on very tall wheels, rib-sided, just one room with a bed at the back, that would today be classed as a Burton-style wagon. He lived in it for a number of years and had a horse to pull it as and when he worked on different farms.

By the early 1960s John had moved on from farm related work to begin working for himself. He was buying and restoring living vans and other horse-drawn vehicles, working out of a rented yard in Esher in Surrey. He travelled about by horse and cart or by bicycle. By 1963 he had sold the first gypsy van and bought a two roomed front entrance Orton showman's van.

Then he found that the yard he had as a base was going to be compulsorily purchased and he was looking for somewhere to relocate. John was invited by the Fairground Society to help in the preparations for the Great Steam Fair that was to take place at Shottesbrooke Park in 1964 and was introduced to John Smith (later Sir John Smith) who offered him a place in Shottesbrooke Park for his caravan and bits and pieces. This was in the spring, prior to the fair scheduled for August.

There is a story that goes around about John Pockett arriving at Shottesbrooke on his bike just with his paintbrushes. Well, it is nearly right. He actually arrived with the bike in the back of a Landrover, which towed his Orton living van up to John Smith's park. John Pockett was involved in helping John Smith find interesting rides and sideshows for the Great Steam Fair. He used to accompany John Smith every weekend, travelling to differ-

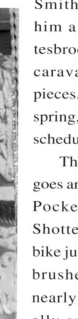

*fig 12*
*Centaur restored by*
*John Pockett,*
*previously in the*
*collection at Wookey*
*Hole*

ent fairs. It was a very special time and after the steam fair he stayed on at Shottesbrooke Park to work on items from John Smith's own collection.

Soon after the Shottesbrooke fair John met a man called Eric Goodey, who had been involved in all aspects of the horse-drawn era, and his brother Harold who had a famous yard called 'The Car Dump'. Goodey's Yard in the 1960s was a mecca – showman's engines with trees growing through, old living vans collapsing in ditches, old buses and cars and horse drawn vehicles – an absolutely wonderful place for John and for many other collectors and restorers in the early days of the preservation movement. If Harold Goodey liked you, you were ok, but otherwise you were not allowed in.

Eric Goodey used to turn up at Shottesbrooke Park about eight o'clock on a Sunday morning, 'Pockett, Pockett, up you get. Bring your brushes.' John would go off in the Landrover to the yard at Hurst, where he would be worked hard using his painting skills. As John says, 'What an education. Anybody who met that man would recognise that he had a tremendous knowledge. I learnt an awful lot from him.'

John worked on everything to do with preservation while there – horse drawn vehicles, old commercial lorries and fairground items.

## At Cookham

Then in 1966 John moved into a yard in Cookham High Street. He was there for a long, long stay, all of 21 years. By 1967, he also had an adjoining antique shop which he named Pockett & Hocketts. At Shottesbrooke he had started undertaking fairground painting and at Cookham he was doing a considerable amount of restoration as well. He has always considered himself a stickler for trying to get things back to as near to original as possible.

John was not formally trained and never seriously went to art school. He had a little help from someone who did gilding of picture frames. Other than that it was learning by talking to people, sometimes just by making mistakes and having to rework and sometimes from people like Neddy Matthews. Neddy introduced him to a number of different fairground painting styles including the use of flamboyant paints and marbling, using a goose feather for graining.

When he moved to Cookham John did work for a number of showmen. He painted Jeff Bach's overboats and did work for Keith Emmett and was beginning to get a name for himself. Colin Thorpe has been another good customer of John's over the years. But the main thing that he has always done most is restoration and painting of showman's and gypsy living vans. That is above all what he believes he will be recognised for doing.

During the late 1970s, John was working in Somerset on restoration of items in the Lady Bangor fairground collection which was then at Wookey Hole. John worked with Alan Brindle who at that time lived at Penn in Buckinghamshire. One of the items John most appreciated restoring was the Orton & Spooner centaur that was in the collection.

While there he thought he would try to find the place where the gypsies were when he was evacuated in the 1940s. John and Alan Brindle found the lane where the cottage was that he had lived in and halfway down the lane he discovered the first group of gypsies had become quite wealthy and had built bungalows. They went further down the lane and John could not believe his eyes. It was almost impenetrable but the gypsy wagons were still there, overgrown with brambles from the hedges. The living van that the old lady had died in was also still there but too covered with brambles for him to reach. He pulled myself up to look inside the one he could reach and said to Alan, 'It looks as though someone is still living in here.' As they looked they saw this person with a great white beard, covered in overcoats, rise up out of a bed and start to shout at them! A farmworker came by on a tractor and said, 'That's old Walter Jowles.' That was the brother who used to ride about on the big white horse when John was evacuated there with his mother thirty years before.

**A personal project**

One long-term project that John has been working on for almost twelve years is the re-creation and rebuild of a horse-drawn juvenile street roundabout. Everybody gives him 'a bit of stick' about it, because it is never ever finished. The ride was made by Halsteads of Sowerby Bridge in Yorkshire and it was typical of their juvenile rides, with two old Renault style motor cars, together with eight tiny Anderson horses.

The ride is a two-abreast and it builds up on a four-wheeled dray. It was in a terrible state when he bought it, being almost just a pattern.

*fig 13*
*Ceiling restoration by*
*John Pockett in*
*Richard Dobson's*
*Birkby living van*

Some of the original parts have been salvaged but mostly it has had to be rebuilt. The whole dray is new, apart from one piece of timber, although it is built to the original pattern. There are cut corners and there are boards that go on the sides when it is being built up, to complete the base, making a full circle eight feet six wide.

When John first acquired it, some of the horses just fell apart when he touched them. He has salvaged four horses and replaced the others with new carved wood animals – a pair of pigs (John has always been fond of pigs) and a pair of carved cockerels. It has cut glass mirror decoration on the centre, brass rods and tin rounding boards and is hand turned. Everybody says it will be too good to use when it is finished! But John is determined to keep it and will probably just use it for film work and special occasions. There are very few rides like it still in existence.

## John's approach to restoration

John's main aim is always to try to get back to as near original as possible. For example, what often occurs when a wooden horse is stripped down is that, as you go down through the many layers of paint, you find the *second* decoration job carried out is actually the finest. The factory original is good, but when the showman had earned some money with the machine

in glass fibre, but even so, he was pleased to be painting and gilding a full set.

Every job is so different. John finds he lives for the current task and then it is over and he is on to the next one. What really sticks out in his

*fig 14*
*Further example of*
*John Pockett's work.*
*This is the ceiling of*
*Colin Thorpe's*
*restored living van. It*
*is lined in a more*
*narrow style than that*
*shown opposite*

and employed a painter and started to put some money back into the ride, that was the best. In those earlier times all showman were trying to out-do one another. So that second coat, especially on horses, was the one with masses of gold, whereas the true original had just the mane that was gilded. One job he was particularly pleased with was when he painted a full set of galloper horses for Mick Goulding. They were

mind is not just the successful jobs but also the many fabulous characters he has met over the years. The older showmen would come to the fair at Cookham and congregate in his yard and tell him that he was doing it all wrong. He recalls when he used to do carriage restoration work for gypsy dealers. 'You had to be on the ball to get your money out of some of those. Showmen, who wanted the best job at the cheap-

41

est price, always paid. The others *nearly* always paid, but none of them ever became enemies.'

## John's collection of signs

John has been a collector of tickets and painted fairground art for many years. He finds he needs them to make the place habitable. When John was at Cookham he purchased a forty foot stall from a relative of the Noyces. The paintwork on it was by George Howard of Southsea and it was signed by him. The boards dated from the 1930s. It had belonged to Nelson Noyce, prior to Jim Noyce. There were animal scenes, jungle scenes, Red Indians, practically everything was on it. He was told by Noyces that King Edward VIII used the shooting gallery at one of the fairs, and left his raincoat on the stall by mistake. So they put up a sign 'Patronised by Royalty'. That was what happened if any member of royalty went within sight of a ride or stall! John says he foolishly sold it and then much later, at one of Relic Design's sales, he bought back three signs which came from it. He thinks those probably cost him more than he had received for the complete stall!

John has a dodgem panel by a famous London painter from before the Hall and Fowle era, named Fred Packer. He was a pavement artist and then became successful with scenic painting work for showmen. It is said that Packer was seriously fond of the drink and that the showman kept him going with that, giving him a few shillings and perhaps a bed in a truck for the night. It is always after people like him die that they say 'Oh, he was a great painter, was old Fred Packer'.

There is a nameplate saying 'Brayshaw and Sons, Yeadon, nr Leeds, Owners' on the wall. It would have been attached to a wagon on the underside sill of a living van where it was not visible. Many of the living vans were supplied on hire purchase agreements and Mr Brayshaw used to go off to the fairs with his father. He would collect the money owing on their wagons at Hull Fair, the last major fair of the year. Brayshaws would not be able to find the showmen in the winter, so Hull Fair, where they would all have taken a living, would be where Mr Brayshaw would go to find them for the last payment of the year.

As John says, 'There's history, I suppose, to every one of my signs here. They are a nice thing to collect, they don't take up a lot of room and they give me a bit of inspiration and I just love it, really. In this business, it's almost like the showman's life, because your work is your hobby and your total interest in life. It's a 24 hour a day thing.'

## Some wagons in John's collection

As this was being written John had three wagons in his workshop. One was a living van with two big doors at one end and an area inside for packing. It was a very rare example of its type and originally would have been drawn by a pair of horses. The wheels would have been much lower than those now fitted so that it could also travel by rail. As soon as showmen started to use lorries, the packing area inside a living van became obsolete and nearly all the wagons then had the bedroom extended into what was previously the packing area.

This style was very much a northern style of living van and John has never seen one in the south of England. He believes it dates from the First World War, maybe just into the 1920s. What is very interesting was that this would be *the* vehicle, the only one the showman had. The stallholder would live in this, he would store his stall, partly hung on the side and part on the roof, elaborate things would be put in the packing area, perhaps the swag and some painted panels, and he would be self supporting. This would be it, for the smaller showman.

Another wagon John had in his barn appeared very ordinary outside but inside it was '*wow*!' There were very fine deep cut glass windows and mirrors. Originally John thinks it was owned by the Shufflebottom family, but Manning of Southsea, who is the Shufflebottom's son-in-law, had it as his wagon for many years. An antique dealer bought it from Mannings and it was in his garden at Gomshall near Guildford. It was beginning to get in a very sad condition and the water was getting in and eventually John managed to purchase it. It was a Philips of Newport wagon, a very well known firm that made good wagons. It was built in 1928 and originally drawn by a steam road engine.

John is often asked to paint the ceilings for

living vans. He has definitely got a name for ceiling panels. The early living vans frequently had scrolled ceilings and he does a lot of that type of restoration work. He tries to encourage customers to bring plywood panels that he can work on, but sometimes they say, 'Oh well, I've got the panels up already.' It is a real neck aching job, then.

At the time of writing John was soon to be moving again. This move will be the first time he has lived in a house since the 1950s. He will have a cottage and 25 acres of hill country. At the moment he has four bantams and three geese but intends to have a horse and a few other animals as well. 'Of course, I'll also have to have a wagon outside!'

# Vicky Postlethwaite

Anyone travelling along the road past the regimental badges carved on the hillside at Fovant in Wiltshire will come to a long low building which has echoes of England's past industry. The Stainer works belonged to Wilf Stainer, who died in 1992. He jointly owned an Orton & Spooner dodgem set with showman Bernard Cole. The Rodeo Switchback ride, which figures large in what follows, was housed in the Stainer workshop during its restoration by Stephen and Vicky Postlethwaite, who live nearby.

Vicky grew up in Bridgwater in Somerset and went to school in West Street, which is where all the stalls are built up when the annual fair comes to the town. A chip stall would be right outside the school gate. When the fair was arriving she and her school chums would stay on over lunchtime to look at all the traditional Orton wagons the showfolk had in those days. She recalls when she was very young going on just two rides because she was a bit frightened of the other faster ones. These favourites were Alfie Whitelegg's gallopers and Cole's gondolas. She traces her deep-seated interest in the fair from that background.

In her childhood, Vicky remembers having hobby horses and toy cars rather than the usual

*fig 15*
*Vicky Postlethwaite at work on the Halstead juvenile ride*

dolls as playthings. Her interest in painting goes back to those early days when she remembers painting her motor cars, plastic farm animals and horses. Then later, her teachers said she was 'good at art' and so it was decided that she should to go to art college. As Vicky says, 'I did a foundation course for a year, but I was just so impatient. I wanted to get out and do practical things all the time – to leave home and earn money and do exciting things.' On her reports it always said, 'Vicky is continually seeking practical applications for her talent', which summed her up completely. She did manage to get an A-level in art, at the lowest grade, having only spent two hours doing the painting composition when most of the students spent three weeks working on it. For the life drawing the model had clothes on and that threw her completely. She could have coped much better if it had been a nude model.

With hindsight Vicky recognises that she could have gained much more from art school. At one stage she was intending to train for window display and still thinks that would have been a suitable career to follow, with varied and exciting prospects. Her first job was going to work for Courtaulds as a package designer, which she soon found was a bit too obscure to allow her to progress as she wanted. She made an attempt to change her career and went after an opening in advertising. The job was going to be in Park Lane, London and offered seven pounds a week. But Park Lane with parents living in Somerset was just too impractical.

**Fairground interests**

Around 1969 she regained her interests in the fair and in particular in fairground organs. She believes it could all be linked back to her schoolday encounters with Alfie Whitelegg's ride in Bridgwater. She started buying records of fairground organs and hitch-hiking round the country to steam rallies. She met her husband Stephen at one of these events. He was running an organ for Brian Oram and it all grew from there. Showman Jimmy Williams' wife Bunch recalls that Vicky and Stephen first met when they went for a ride on Jimmy's gallopers. Bunch remembers that the ride was full and the two were asked to share seats on one of the horses.

As time went on, Vicky came to know a lot

of people in the steam world and started to work with paints again. When she first met Stephen he had a bus, what would be called an 'under restoration' bus (something he tries to keep quiet about these days) and it was painted by Vicky on her honeymoon! Then Stephen and Vicky acquired a Scammell lorry, the *Sir Hilary*, again from the showman and fairground painter Jimmy Williams. It needed something to pull and so they acquired a traditional showman's living wagon. It was a 1934 Brayshaw, in top condition, which was owned by Theodore Frankham. The Frankhams were one of the families that kept things beautifully. They never used to cook or eat in that wagon. When it was bought from Mr Frankham's daughter Amy, she said, 'You'll be the first people to ever eat a meal in that.'

Then the Postlethwaites somehow *inherited* the management of a well-known Marenghi organ that had belonged to Anderton and Rowland from the West Country. Although the organ belongs to the DeVey family, Steve and Vicky have had it on long term loan for twenty years. Until comparatively recently they were having to spend all its earnings on the actual instrument itself and its running costs. In the last few years they have been able to undertake restoration work on the organ proscenium. Some parts of it had previously been touched up with inappropriate materials and Vicky has put this right with suitable repainting and blending in. Now they believe that when it ages it will do so in a uniform fashion and look quite attractive.

Vicky finds that she does quite a lot of marbling work these days, based on techniques learnt from the well-known fairground painter Billy Hall of Hall & Fowle fame. After working with him she decided to go and learn 'proper' marbling and graining as used in the decorative trades and was lucky to get on a course at a building college. It opened a lot of new doors. She had thought that her experience would leave her as an odd one out, but this was far from the case. For a number of years until quite recently she was painting and restoring furniture as well as fairground items. Also she has done wall decorations in houses and pubs, graining and marbling and paint effects, vegetable swags over Aga stoves and suchlike. She found it was pretty exhausting, especially as most of the work was in London. It was no joke trudging round London carrying a selection of tins of paint because her customers didn't know what they wanted.

What Vicky has found is that all the techniques she had acquired often tie in together,

Then in 1976 the Postlethwaites acquired a Halstead juvenile to go with the lorry and organ. It had been in store since 1953 and was in rather a sad state of repair, although it was absolutely

*fig 16*
*Anderton &*
*Rowland's Marenghi*
*organ*

because for example working on the Anderton and Rowland organ was similar to patching up antique painted furniture. All her different skills were involved.

complete right down to the brasso and polishing rags! Stephen and Vicky worked on it evenings and weekends and first presented it in beautiful condition for the 1977 travelling season.

## The Rodeo Switchback

But the real big task came when they acquired the Rodeo Switchback in 1982. It was major 'all-change' then. This ride has a long history, traced back to its ownership by James Pettigrove around the end of the nineteenth century. In 1974 it was exported to the Six Flags Great Adventure Park in New Jersey and, contrary to some reports, they did quite a lot of work on it before eventually abandoning it after there was a change in the ownership of the park. Even with restoration work at the park, the ride suffered from many problems in the USA, with extremes of temperatures and other demands of a busy modern amusement park. When it was eventually abandoned, it would probably have been destroyed but for the action of one employee at the park who kept the parts together.

*fig 17
Stephen & Vicky's Halstead juvenile, complete with Verbeeck organ*

It was brought back to England by a group who named themselves Switchback Ventures, with directors Stephen Postlethwaite, Tim Blyth, Wilf Stainer, Graham Downie and Arthur

Thomson. This group sold shares, mainly to individuals interested in preservation, to raise the funds needed for restoration. On return in 1982 the rear shutters were missing and it was found that the track was not aligned correctly. It was oval not round, and one of the hills was a different height to the other, so it probably kept de-railing. Some of the carved work was also in a poor state and parts were missing.

When the huge ride had to be restored it threw Stephen and Vicky right in at the deep end. That was when Billy Hall came down to stay with them to help out and teach Vicky how to do marbling. He decorated two of the rounding boards and one car and a handrail and then let her carry on. It was real practical tuition. When he was with them he was well past normal retirement and was rather out of date with modern materials. He used to send Vicky off to the shops to get things that had not been produced for years. In some ways that was an advantage, because he'd been out of painting for such a long time and he was in a 'time warp'. The Switchback was more his era, whereas someone like Fred Fowle would have needed to go back in style to paint the switchback in the correct way. Billy Hall was with them for a while and kept saying

*fig 18*
*Rodeo Switchback*

Oh, Vicky, it's such a big job. Are you sure you can do it?' He *knew*! And very soon, so did she.

There were many enjoyable hours spent in the workshop throughout one summer when the ride was ready for painting, with Vicky listening to and learning from Billy Hall. She wishes now that she had a tape recorder going when the conversation turned to Billy's brother Edwin and their years at Orton & Spooners and Lakins. Billy would talk of his brothers skills and also

about the dance band they had formed. Latterly, in his retirement, Billy said he had decided that he wanted to become 'a *real* artist'. He must have been rather like Vicky herself, never having the benefit of professional tuition. He had gone back to evening classes at college on oil painting techniques and was creating copies of Constables to order. They were brilliant and Vicky expects his wife was left with a house full of his 'Old Masters' after he died.

*fig 19*
*Vicky's cowboy scene*
*on rear shutters of*
*the Rodeo*
*Switchback*

51

Vicky recalls going to his house once with part of the new bottom shutters that had to be made for the switchback. It did not turn out to be an entirely satisfactory visit because they soon discovered it was impossible to work out how to paint all of the shutters with only one of them there at his house. Billy tried to draw it out on brown paper, but it was all tongued and grooved boarding, which Vicky says is how everybody thinks it should have been originally. He said, 'you can't paint properly on stuff like that with all those indentations. I'm sure old Sid Howell would never have painted on tongued and grooved boarding.' But she says if you look at the old pictures, it really does look like that. It is terrible to work with as each painted line you make is broken by the grooves every two inches. When you stand the work up all the wet paint runs down the joins in the wood.

Stephen and Vicky, together with a band of helpers were working on that ride for eighteen months before it was able to make its first appearance, its debut at the Great Dorset Steam Fair in 1984. They travelled it full-time for four seasons.

'We were doing it on a shoestring and had all old equipment which made it extremely hard work. We had very few staff compared to what they would have had in the old days to move it. There were only five of us, including me, to build it up. It would take us two days and that was going all day, both days. Then it took a day to pull it down, then two days on the road to the next venue. You never ever stopped, you were going all the time. It was just too much.' They decided to try and do some venues where they could stop for a week or two at a time. Opening at museums like Ironbridge and Wookey Hole was tried, but they found the daily routine staying at one place eventually palls. 'You don't take a great deal of money, just enough to tick-over and pay the staff, which is not enough. The Great Dorset Steam Fair was virtually the only place where we had star billing.'

It was inevitable that the ride had to be sold and it finally went to the UK Fairground Heritage Trust in 1993. According to Vicky, 'We were continuing work on the ride right up to the end. And whoever takes it on now will be continually replacing bits of wood. It just goes on forever – it's forty tons of wood. That's why it's got to be kept inside. The wood you can get nowadays to do repair jobs seems to be inferior in quality. It's not going to last. We used to just put a coat of primer on the wood and then start building up the paint, but you've got to soak it in preservatives now. It certainly slows the process down.'

One lucrative sideline is the use of old-time fair equipment as backgrounds in film work. The Rodeo Switchback was used in Granada TV's *Lost Empires* and also in a film about the bioscope and cinematograph pioneer William Haggar, *A Penny for Your Dreams*. The Postlethwaite's collection has often been used in film work and they have also organised full-size fairs to be brought together for filming by calling on equipment from all over the UK.

**After the Switchback**

Life has been more pleasant for Stephen and Vicky since they parted with the switchback.

Their collection now includes a set of Thomas of Chertsey High Park Swings, a Halstead juvenile complete with Verbeeck organ, a very old Striker with ornate carved work and mirrors, an old side 'joint', a set of small children's swings, a single swingboat and an early coconut sheet. Vicky describes the latter as 'shall we call it a *rustic* coconut shy'. She particularly enjoyed the re-creation of the 1930s look of their 'joint'. At that date the practise was to have simple lining around the panels and small transfer decoration. Vicky's restoration included re-creating the original style of transfer in paint, aiming for exact duplication of the original pansy flower decor.

Stephen and Vicky have also recently acquired an 1840 swingboat, which is just a single boat seating eight people. It is mainly used just for film work. There are very few rides around

*fig 20*

*1840s Odcombe single swingboat*

from such an early period. It has been kept painted in plain colours as appropriate to that early date in order to be accurate for filming work. Vicky says 'It's so sound and in beautiful condition, that it seemed a shame not to grab it when we had the opportunity. We went back to the people we bought it from and found that it was built as a parish amusement, for Sunday School treats. It's known as the Odcombe swingboat, after the village of Odcombe, near Montacute, which is where it was built.

Vicky describes her approach to restoration. 'By the time we acquire these things, they will have been repainted many times. As you remove the layers, sometimes you can find the original factory paint intact. I try to take photos and tracings at each stage to provide a record and help with the final restoration. Reference books of fairground history and art are also a source, plus of course, a lot of practice.'

Vicky likes to do several different styles of painting to fit each item concerned rather than imposing one look on everything. She enjoys the challenge of copying something. 'Perhaps that's my forte – not an immediately recognisable style like Jimmy Williams or Neddy Matthews,

but the ability to add a bit of imagination to a traditional piece of decoration. Perhaps I'm really an *artful faker*. I say to myself, "this is a 1930s joint, let's do a 1930s paint style on it" or "this is a Halstead juvenile, let's copy the paintwork that was done originally on those".

Vicky has recently been doing a project on small scale horses with fairground carver Woody White. They are Woody's design of horse and have a brass pole and a marbled base and the tails are real horsehair. Vicky adds the tails and now she can even get them to hang properly. More recently still she has been working hard painting the children's rides that Woody has carved as the centrepiece for the toy departments of the new *Daisy & Tom* children's stores owned by Tim Waterstone. (refer to the chapter on Woody White)

These days Vicky and Stephen are busy in the summer going from place to place operating their amusements and playing fair organs. They don't have a traditional run of places like most showmen. They try somewhere new and if it's no good they drop it, and if it is, they do it again. It certainly keeps them busy.

# Fairground Carvers

## Woody White

Any showman or fair organ owner in the UK will think instantly of Woody White when they contemplate having any wooden carved work undertaken. Woody's name is synonymous with this aspect of the business to the point where one wonders if this is how his first name appears on his birth certificate. He is widely recognised in the UK for his fairground, organ front and figure woodcarvings and his work has been exported around the world. His business is based near Weston-Super-Mare in Somerset.

### Starting up

Woody started back in June 1987, at first working from his home. The roof height of only six feet six inches soon became an obstacle to progress when he took on the job of making a front for a Page and Howard organ which had to be about nine feet high. Luck was with him when he discovered there were some workshops under construction near his home just at the time the extra space was needed. They were conver-

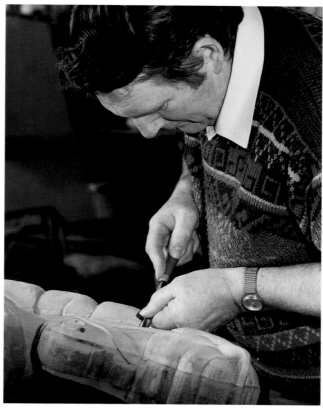

*fig 21*
*Woody White carving a rocking horse in basswood, a wood he uses when lime is in short supply*

sions from farm milking parlours and he put his name down for one straight away.

During 1996-97 Woody was carving panels for an organ front as a 'background' job to all his other work. These were for a new 98-key organ being built for showman Jimmy Noyce. The final piece was an eighteen feet long proscenium top, the design for which was based on a

it had a very plain front, just flat panels and what Woody thought were some rather awful looking storks. He said to the owner Peter Watts as a bit of a joke, 'I'll carve a new front for this for you.'

bioscope carving made for the Harniess family in the early 1900s. The huge carving has two flying horses with their heads and front legs projecting out from the main carved panelwork. This final organ carving is in lime wood throughout and took nine weeks to complete.

Early in his career Woody undertook a carved front for an organ named *Neptunus*. At that time it was owned by Peter Watts but after his death it is now owned and travelled by his widow Jean. When Woody first saw that organ,

Of course he was taken up on the offer and it took Woody two and a half years of his spare time to complete the job. Peter said he wanted something unusual on the theme of Neptune, so Woody created a design that started off with that figure in the centre, then added two big mermaids and the waves across the bottom, and then a whale and a ship. When the drawings for this went to Peter Watts, he said, 'That's nice, but I want twice as much.' Two batches of rocks with seaweed and a lot of clam shells were added to the layout. It finished up with many of the carved parts on the front moving with the music. The two mermaids ride on fishes and wave their arms, with the jaws and fins of the fishes mov-

*fig 22*
*Jim Noyce's organ proscenium with two flying horses, carved in lime by Woody White*

ing as well. Then there are several seagulls and two crabs with moving claws.

People like to sit in front of the organ while they eat their picnics, listening to the music and watching everything that moves. On most organs just the bandmaster and sometimes bell ringers are the only moving things, but on *Neptunus* there are around 28 moving parts. People sit there looking at the cockle shells moving with the different notes and part of the fun is to try and be looking at each shell just at the time

it opens with the next note. *Neptunus* usually beats them at this game!

The first large organ front Woody carved was for Robin May and when the owner came down to see his progress, he said that he also wanted a harlequin carved to go on the front. Virtually all Woody's work comes by word of mouth and additions often arise that way as well. He made the harlequin but sadly Robin May died before the organ front was delivered. It was then sold to Norman Hobbs from West Sussex and he only had it about six months before *he* died. It seemed that there was rather a jinx associated with that organ.

Woody's first trial attempt at carving a

fairground horse is on display on one wall in his workshop and on an adjoining wall is his hundredth horse, suitably named *Centurion*. There is quite a difference between them in the details that really count. Woody recalls that it all began rather casually. 'When I started out, somebody asked me if I could make carousel horses and I just naturally said "yes" without thinking. I had to stop what I was doing to practice and make one, to be sure I could do it.' That first trial taught him a great deal. Looking at it now he believes that its overall shape and size is alright but the mane is wrong, the teeth are wrong and the face is too broad. As well as that, the eyes and ears are wrong – just so many details which are not right that they add up to the animal as a whole being a long way from correct. He had galloper-owner Jimmy Noyce visit to give a critique of it, to tell Woody what was right and what was wrong and help him do better on the next one. Woody remarks, 'You have to listen to people like that who really know what they're talking about. Mind you I've since been offered a couple of thousand pounds for that first one, just because it was the first horse I ever did.' That horse has raised a considerable sum of money for charity, because it used to be taken out and people charged to have their photos taken on it. He reckons that thousands of people must have sat on it. The difference between that first horse and *Centurion* is obvious even to the untrained eye.

Woody estimates that he has now carved about 170 animals, about 120 figures and about 50 complete organ fronts, along with undertaking architectural work, handrail mouldings and restoration of antiques.

### Woody's technical bit

'I nearly always work in lime. It's the woodcarver's wood, hard enough to take a clean cut but soft enough not to blunt the tools. If something's to be polished I'll use white ash, but nearly everything I do is going to be painted after it's carved, so lime is the ideal material.' He dries his wood in his own kilns. If an item is really needed fast, the wood can be matured from the growing tree to being ready-for-use in three months, but as Woody says, it's far better to saw it and let it stand for nine to twelve months to air dry and then just put it in the kiln to finish. A few years ago he and his son bought three 100 foot high trees and had them all sawmilled together. If the opportunity arises he buys in timber as fallen trees after storms. 'But there haven't been opinion is not as nice as English lime to work with because it is a little too soft. He still uses lime for figures and for fine details but uses the

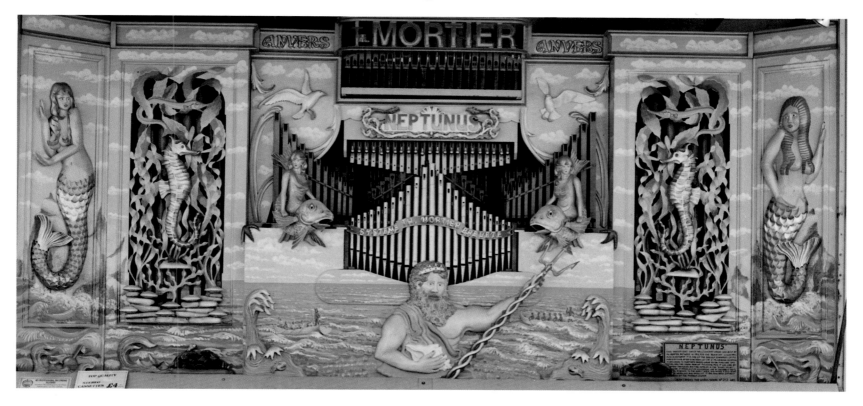

any big storms in the last few years, so there aren't any trees lying around for us to gather up. I could really do with another big storm.' When the right wood is in short supply he resorts to buying in American basswood, which in his basswood for simple scrollwork and larger items.

He carves rocking horses as well as fairground ones and has a preference for carving in the American styles. He rather likes to make

*fig 23*
*Jean Watts Neptunus*
*organ front*

things in other styles than the traditional English ones but of course will do the latter if required by his customers. Woody carves all the trappings of his animals in preference to putting leather on them. He can make an animal such as a full size rocking horse in five days, from the assembled pieces of wood to the work being finished and set on its base. His son puts all the initial wood sections together and does all the sanding work at the finish.

## Some of Woody's output

Woody thinks that one of his most interesting jobs was carving a complete set of twelve outside row galloper horses for James Graham. They were to replace the glass fibre ones that are normally used on his restored set of gallopers up in Scotland. Each horse was carved with different shields of Scottish knights on its side. Neddy Matthews carried out all the painting on them (see chapter on Jimmy Graham).

One commission of Woody's was to make a seven foot long lion and a seven foot dragon for a lawyer in New York. The lion was made to go in his office but when that was being refurbished it temporarily went into his lounge at home.

When the office was finished his wife would not part with the carving, so the dragon was commissioned to keep it company.

Woody also remembers a customer he has from Melbourne, whose first order was for a bandmaster figure for a Wurlitzer organ. Then he had a bear made as a kitchen seat and then a cat to go on the other side of his kitchen table. Recently there followed an order for two carved ladies and an Australian Father Christmas. Closer to home, he carved the show top for Richard Dean's replica bioscope and the replacement front for the Hooghuys organ that was badly burnt in the 1991 fire at the organ collection of Teddy Reed.

Woody goes to steam rallies and some of the major craft fairs held throughout the summer. In order to have work to display and hopefully to sell at these events, he carves items as speculations during spare time in the winter. When attending shows, Woody's aim is to ensure that he is always carving something big and impressive. 'If I can do a full-size galloper, all the better, or maybe a middle size rocking horse. I'm pleased to say that some people that really do want a *good* rocking horse are prepared to

*fig 24*
*Centurion horse in*
*Woody White's*
*workshop*

pay a realistic price for one.' Occasionally he has special commissions, usually for collectors, to produce something different to the normal type of animal, maybe a shire horse or a unicorn. With the right timing they all get done as part of the show. But Woody often hears remarks at these shows and rallies from people who, because maybe they've done a little carving perhaps fifteen years ago, try to tell him that he is doing it all wrong! 'People these days do seem

*fig 25*
*Children's store*
*juvenile carved by*
*Woody White and*
*painted by Vicky*
*Postlethwaite*

to be much more intent on criticising than being supportive and appreciative.'

Sometimes there is a one-day carving demonstration to be done at one of the shows. In order to tackle an item where the final result is needed in the day, Woody might undertake a full-size galloper head but only two inches in width. That's something which can be done quite easily in six or seven hours. On another occasion he might undertake a much larger project. Once he spent two weekends working on a lion, first at Netley Marsh Steam Rally and for the second weekend at Heddington & Stockley Rally. He organised an announcement over the public address system: 'A lion has been spotted up near the craft tent and please be wary when approaching that area.' It really brought the crowds over to see him finishing the piece.

He also undertakes restoration work. One project he particularly remembers was a Savage dobby horse dating from about 1860 or 1865. 'It was in a hell of a state. We took about 25 coats of paint off and when we reached the second coat of paint that was on there, it must have been a very cheap and nasty, because it all powdered as it came off. The original design could be seen stained into the wood and it was possible to recreate it.' He had to replace the ears and part of the neck and although the mane was virtually all there, the belly board had to be replaced and so did two of the legs. It was all solid wood again when he had finished. He put a new hair tail on it. In all twelve parts were replaced and when finished Woody believes

*fig 26*
*Cockerel on juvenile ride, carved by Woody White and painted by Vicky Postlethwaite*

it was exactly as it would have looked when it first came out of the maker's paint shop.

In the mid-1990s Woody White was carving some small horses for Vicky Postlethwaite to paint and sell. They sold about twelve of the English ones, but the one American design he did remained unsold so Woody gave that to his wife. He thinks that American style horses do not sell over here and vice versa.

A very interesting new commission came his way in 1997. It came about after a chance meeting at the Stanton Drew steam rally in 1996 where Woody was demonstrating some of his work. He was asked to quote for a complete wooden carved children's roundabout which was to be an attraction in the first of a chain of new children's stores with the brand name *Daisy and Tom*, which opened in Chelsea, London in July 1997. It is ten feet in diameter and has ten animals, six horses and four cockerels. There are carved centres with mirrors and carved rounding boards. The ride was painted by Vicky Postlethwaite and completed in May 1997 and a second roundabout for the *Daisy and Tom* store in Manchester followed.

# Robert Race

Looking for another carver working in the UK in the fairground area is somewhat of a problem. There are several who advertise as carvers of rocking horses and occasionally a name comes up as having carved a set of galloper horses more as a one-off venture. Liz Mangles, who carves new wood animals for Colin Jones' gallopers and other rides is an example of this. Also there are those who carve miniature horses for their working model fairground rides. Ernest Summerhayes, who is constructing a 1/12th scale model based on Noyce's gallopers is an excellent example in this group. Someone who has carved the animals for his own operating juvenile ride, some of which are quite exotic and who is more closely involved with the fairgound scene has been selected here.

Earlier in his career Robert Race was a school biology teacher. Then he worked as an administrator at a teacher centre, but was becoming dissatisfied and decided to make a career change. He started making dolls houses and miniature furniture and then branched out into making moving wooden toys of various kinds. He just learnt as he went along without having had any formal training, but there was probably something he had inherited to guide him along. Robert's father was an industrial designer of furniture so he was brought up in an environment where people were designing and making things and as a result he had always been making things himself since an early age.

Robert constructs a wide range from simple moving toys for children, up to wooden structures that he describes as simple automata, which are much more aimed at adults. Recycled wood is used in many of his toys. He is a member of the British Toymakers Guild and exhibits in galleries and puts on shows based on his moving objects. He finds this whole genre is a very popular one today.

## The Halstead ride

Robert has always been interested in fairground-related items, fairground 'stuff'. In the autumn of 1985 he was looking for a project to

*fig 27*
*Robert Race working*
*on a batch of toys*

glass fibre. It was a working ride in that you could turn the handle and it went round but it obviously hadn't been decorated for years. Although Robert had really gone with a friend just as an onlooker, he finished up by buying the ride. His wife Thalia didn't believe him when they returned home and his friend told her that they had actually bought a ride!

Robert's first interest was in restoration, with the objective of actually taking the ride out to events. It lacked many of the animals and he was very interested in the prospect of carving and painting new ones to populate it. He started by learning about the specifics needed to restore and complete the ride in the appropriate style. He could see it as a very nice ride in his minds eye but it needed stripping down and reworking from scratch. It was all carefully stripped off but there was absolutely nothing underneath as an original pattern to work from and restore. At this point Robert researched into fairground ride history to support the work. There was not any history to the actual ride that he had acquired except that he thinks it had last been used in Lincolnshire. The cars had the number plate WD1943 painted on them. WD, meaning War

undertake and went to a sale of antiques at a farm near Malmesbury, where Relic Designs used to have a regular annual event. Amongst the miscellaneous lots there was a Halstead juvenile ride. There were the two original metal motor cars that Halstead normally had on their rides but only four other animals, these being in

*fig 28*
*Robert Race's*
*Halstead juvenile ride*

Department, followed by the year, seemed to suggest that it probably had not been painted since the Second World War. He stripped the paint layers back carefully to see what was underneath and found the cars were quite inter-esting as they had been repainted several times and nicely lined out at each stage, just in a plain and simple style. The rounding boards, as far as he could tell, had never had anything really in-teresting on them at all. There were no original animals on the ride, just the four glass fibre horses, so there was no way of knowing what the originals would have been like. Robert looked at photographs and went to Wookey Hole to see the collection that was there at that time. Tim Barker, a showman from Bristol who had done restoration work on the collection was very helpful. He explained about flamboyant and other fairground paints and told Robert where they could be obtained in Bristol.

So he got to work, starting by making some design sketches, all out of his head. He thought up the slogan to go round the rounding boards, as saying 'Robert Race's Famous Juvenile Arena of Ponies, Poultry, Myths and Motor Cars' and that set the scene for the animals that were needed. He made drawings for the more unusual items like centaurs and sea-horses but started the actual carving with a straightforward pony. Quite by chance, some friends of Robert's had inherited a very old carved adult pony of around 1880 date, which had come from a ride that had been burnt when in storage in Wiltshire. His friend had acquired the one animal and kept it in his garage for years. When they finally decided they weren't going to do anything with it

they passed it on to Robert. It needed a couple of new legs and the top of its head was missing. He took it completely apart, carved the replacement parts needed and put it back together again.

The first animals for the Halstead were made by just copying that horse to a smaller scale. Robert used woods that he had to hand at the time, hardwood for the legs and a pine box for the body. It was certainly not the ideal wood for carving, but this first animal was such a simple form, without any detail on it, that it was fairly straightforward to carve.

In order to operate the ride when first acquired, it was completed by buying two glass fibre Orton & Spooner style cockerels to add to the four ponies that came with the ride so as to complete the ring of animals, together with the two cars. As soon as Robert had the rounding boards painted he travelled to events and opened to the public. Its first outing in Robert's ownership was to a fete at Sherston, in Gloucestershire in 1986.

Being a designer and carver, Robert was interested in replacing the glass fibre animals and adding more carved detail as he progressed further with the ride. It took him several years to complete the full set of animals that he had en-visaged. Plans for the more interesting creatures gradually took shape. Robert carved two of the simple wooden ponies first, then he created the much more complicated sea-horses, always making two at the same time. Lime wood was used for much of the sea-horses, although again the basic structure was a pine box. He looked at the books – Weedon and Ward's *Fairground Art* being a particular reference, and again he went to look at what he could see already travelling and at the Wookey Hole Collection. There were plans to create two centaurs next but he and his wife were both struck by an Orton & Spooner dragon in *Fairground Art*. There was a two-seater example in the Wookey Hole collection, which was helpful. It was a magnificent beast, like a horse with scales on and a strange mouth with a tongue hanging out. Robert made a scaled-down version of that. It was quite a com-plicated carving and it took a while to do, learning as he went along. In 1995 he carved and painted the centaur to complete the set of ani-mals envisaged. The last things carved were some crown boards, which he recognises were probably never fitted to the original ride. Now

he would like to put mirrors in the centre. As he remarks, 'The Halstead has been a one-off for me. It's fitted in with other things that I do and I've been able to keep adding to it, keeping it on the go over the years.'

**Travelling the ride**

The ride takes Robert and Thalia to some in-teresting events. They particularly enjoy being at festivals where there is no fairground as such. 'We always do better in those circumstances, because obviously, you've got less competition. If you can find an event like that, it can go very well.' They also do local school fetes and simi-lar events, some of which are good and some of which are a lot of hard work for very little re-turn. It is hard work if they have to put the ride up and take it down again in an afternoon, not like putting up one of the modern fold-out hy-draulic rides, but given the right event, they can achieve a good return from it. Of course it is al-ways *so* dependent on the weather. Usually it is just Robert and Thalia who work the ride, plus sometimes a few friends that they can call on if necessary.

In the nature of things the animals get a fair

*fig 29*
*Robert Race's carved*
*sea-horse*

amount of knocking about and have to be re-touched regularly. Robert recalls a terrible event about three years ago when they hit a pothole whilst driving and the rack with all the wooden animals came off the back of their trailer. There was considerable damage and several broken

*fig 30*
*Robert Race's carved*
*dragon*

hooves. But one of the beauties of wood is that it is quite simple to cut new parts and just dowel and glue them on.

He is very impressed with the way the rounding boards have lasted because they have not been re-painted at all since first travelling the ride. The flamboyant lacquer, although it fades slightly, still looks pretty good. He did all the lettering himself, 'That was part of the fun of doing it, learning to do all the different things.' He wishes the manufacturers had not changed their flamboyant lacquers, the new amber in particular not having the same depth as its predecessor. He likes the various lacquer effects, but also mentions that using gold leaf would be wonderful, except that it stands out so much that it has to be all or nothing.

Their experience is that the ride entertains children up to about the age of eight. Above eight there are problems because it is just not exciting enough. Two year olds are very happy on it and if they are not too busy at an event they let any mothers with little babies on the ride.

The events where there can be problems tend to be those where there is not enough for the children over about eight to do. The net result it that those older ones come on the ride and find it does not give them the thrills they want. So they start using it as a climbing frame and moving from animal to animal and jumping on and off. That means it becomes dangerous for the smaller children – they copy the older ones and also they may get landed on. So they always dread if they go somewhere and can see that there is not enough for older children to do. Other than that it's great fun.

All the animals are single seaters, so it is a bit tricky with mums and babies. Mothers very often want to go in the cars and they discover there is no room for their legs although some manage to do it with a squash. Robert does not encourage that unless they are not at all busy. They have had to learn by experience. 'Safety really comes down to observation, and you have to have eyes in the back of your head! With the right age range there isn't any real problem. It's a stable ride and with hand turning is not going very fast.'

It will keep two to eight year olds happy all day long. Robert and Thalia really notice *that* when they go to a pay event where they are giving free rides. 'It's hard work then!'

# Fair Organs

## Andrew Whitehead

Andrew Whitehead has been building fairground organs since the mid-1970s. He first started by undertaking contract work for Chiappa of London, building at his workshop near Stratford-upon-Avon, where he has always lived. His wife Jean is also involved in the business, cutting organ book music. In 1980 they decided to go and work directly for the Chiappa company. Victor Chiappa was a very Victorian gentleman in his outlook. The Whiteheads found him very set in his ways and difficult to work for so they came back to Stratford and started their own organ business.

That was in 1981 and they have been going ever since, riding out the ups and downs of recessions along the way. They undertake everything to do with fair organs – constructing new ones, rebuilding, repairs, tuning, music, virtually everything apart from carving and painting of organ fronts. Andrew undertakes all the mechanical construction and the setting-up aspects of the work involved. As he remarks, 'Creating the right voice and balance of sound from an organ is the difficult part. It's one thing to make a rank of pipes, but making them sound like one instrument, one choir, that's the hard bit'.

### Andrew's range of organ work

Andrew Whitehead manufactures organs from the 30-key size up, the smallest that he considers sensible from a musical viewpoint. At the upper end, the biggest one at the moment that he looks after is the Wonderland organ in Birmingham, which was once owned by the well-known showman Pat Collins. 'That's 98-key, but it's a big organ with it. It's got more in than other 98-key organs I know. The only one that I know would beat it in terms of the amount of pipes is the White Brothers one.' The Whites organ is really 112-key with a 98-keyframe fitted, which means that there are some parts that have been taken out to make the conversion, but physically what people see from the front is a full 112-key organ. If they know about mechani-

73

cal organs people can count the ranks of violins alone and find there are more than you have in an average 98-key organ. It is considered to be a unique instrument.

Andrew tries to perpetuate the make of instrument associated with Charles Marenghi of Paris. His customers are private individuals, mainly working or retired businessmen with the interest and the resources to afford a new organ or a major rebuild – people who have *caught the bug*, as it were. They have one or two showmen on their books, one or two of the few that are left still travelling with fairground organs. But the Whiteheads have doubts what the showman-related business will be like in ten years time because Andrew believes that when the next generation takes over they will soon sell any of the old rides that they still have.

*fig 31*
*Andrew Whitehead in his workshop*

## Jim Noyce's 98-key organ

During 1997 Andrew was completing the large 98-key organ that he had been making for Jimmy Noyce as a background fill-in job between organ rebuilds for the last few years (already mentioned in the chapter on Woody White). What makes any organ large, in addition to the number of keys are the extras that are incorporated, fitted in drum stands on either side. Noyce's organ is a four drum stand type, which means there are two wings at each end of the standard centre section. The percussion goes into the bottom of the drum stands instead of

being in the top as normal, to allow all the pipes that are needed over and above those in the centre section to go in the top. Jimmy Noyce says he is buying it because he wants an organ himself, to listen to. 'I don't care if I never take it out. I can go down to my boathouse and switch it on and have my own concert.' Mr Noyce wanted a

reproduction as near as could possibly be made to the Marenghis of Harniess and Goldthorpe Marshall and that is what he is going to have with this one.

Marenghi organs are basically all very similar in layout, but the extras on the ends alter them totally and distinguish one from another. Jim Noyce's one will have considerably more than the standard Marenghi. There will be 50 cello pipes added each side, plus brass trumpets and wooden trumpets to complete the full 98 scale. Then there will be a full percussion set – sleighbells, glockenspiel, side drum, wood block, base drum, triangle and castanets. As for organ figures, Marenghi just had a single organ figure, the bandmaster, and that is all there will be on this instrument.

Jim Noyce is also having an elaborate and

*fig 32*

*Jim Noyce's 98 key organ under construction*

75

deeply carved front, which Woody White has made. That top has been very difficult and in order to achieve the right dimensions it has had to be scaled from original photos of the Harniess organ. Andrew has been able to help because he can work out the actual length that some of the organ pipes in the photo must have been to have the right notes. 'I must say that Woody has done a marvellous job, very good work.'

### Learning the job

Andrew considers that he has had as good a grounding as can be obtained in this day and age, because there is just no-one at all now who can teach these things. He was taught the rudiments of making reed pipes by a Birmingham organ builder. He says, for example, that there are so many ways and means of making what looks like the same pipe, so many very subtle adjustments that, when they are all put together, make a *vast* difference to the sound.

Gavioli had dozens of skilled people in their factory, some of whom they had employed from the biggest church organ manufacturers in Paris. They had years of experience and ideas of modifications to make to any instrument. Anyone that knows the church organ builders that are left will recognise that they are extremely skilled people. They can tell exactly what an organ is going to sound like while it is still a drawing on a piece of paper. They know how to tackle the dozens and dozens of problems that arise in pipemaking alone and unless you have had an apprenticeship and been taught this you cannot really say you are a professional. It takes a long, long time to learn all the information needed and hold it in your head. Andrew still feels he is an amateur in comparison.

### A historical outline

Music on the fairground all started long before the days of steam. At one stage there would be a man walking round playing a penny whistle to attract custom. Then there was a man turning a barrel organ and when steam-driven rides came along an ancillary engine could be fitted to the centre engine to provide power to compress air for the fair organs we still have today. Up until 1892 all fair organs were barrel operated, but after that date book organs took over. Gavioli & C$^{ie}$ and Limonaire & C$^{ie}$, both of Paris, were the major European makers.

Probably nothing distinguishes the various organ styles to members of the general public but the main distinctions between what became the two major makers, Gavioli and Marenghi, is the sound and the layout of the organ. Gavioli had a design which dated back to the barrel organs, which they altered very little right up until their business finished by the time of World War One. Marenghi first started by working for Gavioli, but it is believed that the latter's unwillingness to take on new ideas was one of the reasons why Marenghi left them in 1900. He was full of good new ideas and after leaving he generated further ideas forced upon him through having to work around patents that Gavioli had registered. Andrew considers that the net result of having to get around these patents was that Marenghi actually made a much better instrument.

It is said that Marenghi made more organs between 1902 and 1920 than Gavioli made between 1820 and 1915. Marenghi was doing very well up until his death in 1919 and then the Gaudin brothers, who were the works managers, carried on until 1929. By then there was competition from electric recordings that were coming in. Nobody wanted to carry around great heavy instruments and pay a man to look after them when they could have what was seen then as a small unit, which was called a 'panatrope', in the paybox and do it all themselves. There would be a stack of 78rpm records in place of cumbersome books of music.

Andrew's view is that Marenghis were top quality organs from a mechanical point of view and they produced the excellent instruments that can still be heard today. Looking into Marenghi key frames are to him just like looking into a top quality pocket watch. They are vastly different from Gavioli ones. 'You've got to try and get into the mind of these people, and think about why they did what they did. It was not, "That's a good idea, we'll knock that up." They obviously talked it all through and came up with the best design you could get for the price.' In their day Marenghi were even building using a simple type of production line. Not quite like cars, as far can be ascertained, but by having a number of parts made in advance and put on one side. These would then be picked off the shelf to go into the instrument that each particular customer required. The organs might be going into amusement rides, skating rinks or dance halls. The English market was only a small proportion of Marenghi's work and the company mainly

*fig 33*
*Ayers 89-key Gavioli*
*on their gallopers*

made dance organs for sale in France, Northern Italy, Spain, Belgium, America and the UK. Not so many went to Germany because they had their own makers there.

Gavioli and Marenghi apparently both had spies in each other's works to see who might be copying what. Marenghis used to adjust their keyframe so finely that it would not play Gavioli music properly. All those kinds of practices were going on.

## Chiappa

As far as England was concerned, Victor Chiappa was certainly *the* organ man. He was involved from the age of 20 until he died in 1993 at the age of 92. His father and grandfather knew Gavioli very well. Chiappa were Gavioli agents in the UK. Victor's grandfather worked for Gavioli and then around 1860, he went to America. That was not a success so he came back to England and set up a business in Clerkenwell. In the early days they made barrel organs and pianos for public houses and then moved to book organs. Victor had an extremely

good memory and could relate things quite clearly that happened before the First World War. He was the last person alive that went to Marenghi's funeral. After the First World War the Gavioli business had closed down and there were still new organs needed in the UK at that time, as new rides that required organs were still being made.

From around the 1900s, organs grew bigger and bigger until they culminated in the Gavioli

*fig 34*
*White's 112-key*
*Gavioli, converted to*
*98 key*

110/112-key size. If anyone stands in front of the White's organ, they will find that it does not hurt their ears, as no pipe organ will, but it really is very powerful. What Andrew remembers when he first heard that organ was that it vibrated the turf under his feet.

Chiappa undertook a great deal of organ conversion work in order to standardise the musical scales. There were so many of these at one time that no one could afford to cater for them all. They tried to standardise to three scales: 46/48, 87/89 and 98. One or two of the organs did slip through the net as there are about four 65-key ones around, but apart from that the conversion programme was quite a success. Converting an instrument normally means reducing the key size. The overall size of the case is the major constraint, so it is much easier to take parts out and rearrange the rest than it is to make additions. Pipes are physically taken out and the remaining pipework is rearranged to suit the revised scale.

Fair organ scales are not chromatic, except in the case of the 106/110/112-key ones. All the others omit certain sharp notes from the scales present in the instrument. Also each of the scales are different to one another. Sometimes organs convert well, as they say, and other times, not so well. The question is whether the downward conversion can be reached without producing an instrument that is out of balance or ugly both in appearance and sound.

**Verbeeck**

Verbeeck from Belgium are another firm that have survived right through from the early days of mechanical organs. Johnny Verbeeck is still making organs today (see the later chapter featuring the Eden Palais salon carousel restoration). Their main line at the height of organ production in the early 1900s and between the two World Wars was organs for cafes and dance halls. There was a brother Jimmy Verbeeck that came over to England and set up his business in Islington in London. It is said that every man that was sacked from Chiappa went straight round to Islington, where Verbeeck took him on, and vice versa in some cases.

The early business for Verbeecks was for shop and cafe organs in Belgium and Holland, which would have been installed to replace small orchestras. They were different machines from fair organs in that what was required was something that could be listened to while still carrying on a conversation. So the organs had different pipework, without batteries of reed pipes.

There were also several small organ builders in the UK. The largest were probably the Varetto Brothers in Manchester. Peter Varetto worked at the factory owned by Gavioli that they had in Manchester and then started his own business there. That firm finished during the 1920s depression when business became very scarce. Later, Ben Varetto went to work for Chiappa and continued there right into the 1950s.

The organs Andrew has had in his workshop to be stripped down all have signatures in them. The history of each organ can be traced back from that. 'If you know what to look for, you can more or less see who has changed what, over the years.' Recently he was renovating the organ from Forrest's gallopers and the history of that one could be traced right back to 1901. One thing that has to be watched for is that many French organ makers used fine papers for lining that came from old discarded accountancy ledgers. These were greatly sought after for the quality of the paper. Sometimes people may think that they have an organ that is much earlier that it really is, because they have looked at dates on the lining paper that have had accounts written on them many years before the organ makers used the actual paper in the organ.

## Some favourites

Andrew Whitehead's favourite organ style is the violin-baritone system. He thinks that is very listenable and has got everything you want for the ordinary English fair organ.  One instrument that he says stands up above all else is Teddy Reed's Marenghi with the sleighbells. Horace Holmes, who worked for Chiappa for many years, worked on that instrument and did all the voicing. The sound from that organ is his balance and his voicing. Andrew thinks the sound of that instrument is as good as you will get out of any English fair organ. As he rightly says, 'They are not concert organs, they are *noise makers*. You take the biggest noise maker ever made, the Anderton & Rowland 98-key Marenghi. You can hear that from two miles away.' Done purely to attract the punters on a fair, they were not designed to sit in front of and think, *how delightful*. Steve and Vicky Postlethwaite have that Anderton & Rowland organ on long term loan from the DeVey family and have put an immense amount of time, effort and money into its operation and maintenance. As he says, 'It is a good job there are keen people like them about otherwise these instruments would have all been sent up in smoke a long time ago.' Sadly a lot of them were.

Perhaps that is why there is 'organ mania' these days. People cannot get an 'original', although of course none of them are *true* originals, as they have all been rebuilt or altered. Instead they have a new one made. Andrew has some strong views about how well many of these stand up in comparison to the *originals*.

What many people forget in this country was that the fair organ was made to either go in a bioscope front or in the middle of a roundabout. A roundabout would have its canvas tilt and the ride itself would act like a giant fan, giving movement to the air. So an organ in a set of gallopers is not at all like an organ in the back of a lorry, which can bake out on a hot day. Fair organs are wooden instruments and require a degree of moisture. Also on a very hot day, the air that enters the organ blower gets even more dried up and the result is that the air in the organ has got no 'value' to it, no strength. Some people try to combat this with damp cloths to add moisture to air entering the organ, with partial success, but the general result is to affect the 'speech' of pipes and more drastically the amount of reserve pressure in the organ reservoir. Andrew's firm view is that that is the time when they should be switched off, because otherwise the wood gets cracked. Some of the organs he has had to deal with have the wood shrunk to such an extent that the seams have opened to the point where they would not go back. The only option he has then is to take the instrument apart and re-seat everything and possibly make drastic alterations to critical tolerance parts. He is concerned by the damage which can be done to these instruments, which are his lifelong love.

Andrew is a true artisan, a craftsman that insists on achieving the finest quality within

*fig 35*
*Teddy Reed's*
*sleighbell Marenghi*

price constraints. Everyone can look forward to the completion of the new organ for Jim Noyce as a pinnacle of Andrew's achievements. We all hope that other examples of his large key size instruments will appear on the fairgrounds in the future.

SOME  OPERATING  FAMILIES

# Some Operating Families

## Jack Schofield

Jack Schofield has always worked for himself, right from leaving school when he was seventeen. He originally worked in the electrical contracting business, where he reached the stage of having a retail shop and eleven men working for him. When aged 41, Jack says that he had a 'mid-life crisis' and decided that that was not the way he wanted to go. He believes that life has to be lived in a way, that where an opportunity arises, there comes a time where you have to take a risk.

Jack took his risk when he acquired his first set of gallopers. He didn't know if they were going to earn any money, he just felt the travelling life was something he wanted to do. He had talked to a lot of people involved and just knew he would like the life. So the foreman who had been with him a long time took over the electrical contracting business, the retail shop went to one of the men that used to work for him and Jack finished up 'playing roundabouts' full time.

At that time he had also met his future wife Judith. He reckons it was quite a shock for him, to get married. By the time he was 41, Jack didn't think he was going to find anybody that was willing to get involved with him and his gallopers. 'It's a bit specialised, is this. It's a different sort of life.'

Jack has always lived in the Retford area of Nottinghamshire. In about 1910, his grandfather was a sugar-mouse maker, making pink sugar mice and other similar treats. He lived in the Sheffield area. Jack's mother and father were market gardeners and they grew chrysanthemums and tomatoes as their main crop. Before World War Two his father had a mobile greengrocery shop with which he travelled round the Nottinghamshire colliery villages selling vegetables to the housewives. During the war his father grew onions for the army. They would not let him join up because growing onions counted as a reserved occupation!

### How Jack began travelling

The first thing associated with his interest in travelling that Jack bought was an old caravan, back in 1971. He had gone to have a look at it on a dark evening, not really the ideal time, because you cannot see what you're buying. It was painted a dirty brown colour and was covered with hardboard on the outside and his first reaction was that it did not look at all like what he wanted. Then the person who was selling it opened the door and shone his torch inside. The light hit the mirror opposite the door and the whole van lit up, as if it had been set on fire. The light from that mirror reflected off another one behind the door and then it reflected everywhere. Jack was absolutely amazed and was so taken with it that he bought it then and there.

After that he was looking for something of the right vintage to tow it around. Jack saw an old chain drive Scammell advertised in the *World's Fair*. It was being sold by Bunny Smith, who was a Yorkshire traveller who had a bingo stall. Jack remembers it cost him £420, which was a lot of money back in 1971.

Jack then started going to rallies with his caravan and Scammell in the early 1970s, helping people put up their round—abouts. One of these was a children's ride belonged to a Bill Armitage, who lived near Rotherham and stored it in his coalhouse. Later,

*fig 36*
*Jack Schofield*

Bill was not very well and did not want to take the ride out, so Jack borrowed it from him. He would have to go to Rotherham early on a Saturday morning, load it out of the coalhouse into the van, bring it all the way back to Retford, go to a garden fete or some other 'do' with it, make the money with it and then take it back to Rotherham at six or seven o'clock at night and put it back in the coalhouse again.

He did that for a while and realised there was potential business to be had. So he bought and travelled his own juvenile ride until 1979, which is when the Ashley gallopers came up for sale at auction. The mechanics on the Ashley set were in such good order mainly because, in about 1934/5, the Ashley family had bought a new

Noah's Ark. The only time that their gallopers went out after that was to the Goose Fair and the St Anne's Flower Show at Nottingham. From 1935 until it was used for wartime holiday-at-

*fig 37*
*Jack's ex-Ashley gallopers at Fairford rally in 1996. Judith Schofield is on the ride platform*

home fairs, and then after the war until the '60's, when the rallies started, that ride was only used twice a year.

Jack bought it and worked on its restoration,

all the time selling cars and lorries that he had acquired previously, in order to have money to carry on with work on the gallopers. The first year he took them out was 1983. The first official opening, apart from a 'do' they had at Retford in October the previous year, was to Butterly Railway Museum near Derby, for the May Day Bank Holiday. That was when he realised that railway customers and galloper customers are different people altogether! The only time they took any money was when the trains came into the station. As Jack says, 'Then it was one ride and you'd to wait another hour until the next train came! No good for business at all.'

Luckily, one or two people from other parts of the country came to see, because it was a ride that hadn't been travelled for a while. They wanted Jack to take the ride to Astle Park, which is the other side of Macclesfield. He still only had the chain-drive Scammell tractor. He just looked on the map and forgot about the hills in between Nottinghamshire and there! So he said 'yes'. It was a horrendous journey, especially going across the 'Cat and Fiddle' pass with the box truck and the centre truck behind the Scammell.

When they opened at Astle Park Jack thought the business would be like it had been on his own side of the country. He thought they would just be plodding on, with about 40 pounds of steam pressure. On the Saturday afternoon they were absolutely inundated and nearly took more money in an hour than they had taken the whole previous season. As Jack says, 'I hadn't got enough steam on it. I was having to push it round on the inside on the brasses to get the ride started. I couldn't believe it. We must have had 80 people on it each time.'

What had happened was that the year before, many rallies in the North West had lost their gallopers. Dormans from Nottingham had travelled that part of the country and they had missed a year. The organisers of these rallies were looking for a replacement and luckily Jack came on the scene at just the right time.

Every year brings its own problems as well as its good times. Jack remembers one year when the machine tester came and said 'There's been a chimney failure on a set of gallopers and we're going to check all the chimneys now.' The trouble with galloper chimneys is they rot on the inside, not the outside. There can be no obvious sign of trouble from the outside, which can still look perfect. Jack was up at the top of the chimney and the tester asked him to just bring a wood chisel and scrape the paint off so that he could get a proper reading from his ultrasonic tester. Jack was scraping away when there was a bump and the chisel went straight through the chimney!

Jack had to contact his supplier for a replacement tube. 'Now the trouble is it's imperial size tube of course and nowadays the only place you can get English imperial size tube is Germany!' That replacement had to be imported specially and machined up with the help of a local engineering firm. The next year Jack checked the bottom part of the chimney and two years later he had to replace that, which was an even bigger job as all the gears had to come out. 'It's a case of having to spend money every winter. Like any machine, it needs maintenance and you've got to keep up with it.'

Running repairs are called for on other things than the gallopers. One year when they were coming back from Bishops Castle after August Bank Holiday the chain-drive Scammell jammed up on the old A5 Shrewsbury ring road. The drive went to the back wheels, and Jack just stopped. What had happened was that a wheel hub had cracked round. On a chain drive, the cogs for the drive are on the outside of the brake drum and the brakes are on the inside. Suddenly it wouldn't drive anything and the brake wouldn't work either. The only way he could stop was to lock up the draw bars. There they were in an L-shape right across the A5 on a Bank Holiday Tuesday afternoon, just as all the holiday makers were coming back from Wales.

The caravan and the pick-up that were supposed to be following them had gone wrong somewhere. The driver thought Jack was in front of him and he drove all the way to Retford. Back in Shrewsbury, Jack sat on the pavement waiting for a breakdown truck when a police motorcycle man came along. Jack could hear him on his radio saying, 'Oh well, that's the west side of Shrewsbury blocked up' and then, 'that's the Whitchurch side blocked' and everything

*fig 38*
*Double-seater Orton*
*& Spooner horses on*
*Jack Schofield's*
*gallopers. These were*
*carved in 1925 when*
*the ride was upgraded*
*from a 'dobby' set*

got completely blocked up for three and a half hours. They were having to divert traffic through housing estates.

When the breakdown lorry came, the driver would not take all three vehicles together. They were stuck in Shrewsbury all night, with no caravan. Jack slept in the box truck, with the covers that pack the horses pulled round his arms and legs and the lad that was with him slept in the Scammell cab. There wasn't a window in

*fig 39*
*Double-seater Orton*
*& Spooner horses on*
*Jack Schofield's*
*gallopers*

one side of that cab and there was a frost that night.

So at the end of that season Jack ploughed the money he had earned into better transport. The next year he had a newer Scammell, which went a little faster and so he could go a little further. He decided then that whatever happens, the caravan would be towed behind, so that if anything went wrong there would be somewhere to sleep, something to eat and somewhere to make a cup of tea. He had his little 14ft Sprite caravan on the back of the centre truck and that was how he travelled, right through until he was married.

Jack bought the living van he has now for he and his wife Judith to live in. When it first came it was in a very poor state. None of the kitchen was there, the window frames were rotten and the roof leaked. They worked on the van all the winter before they were married, which was on April 5th 1986, just before they went to the Bass Museum at Burton-on-Trent for May Day. That is how he started. From then on it has been a case of working, earning a bit and spending a bit.

### The Gavioli organ

There was no music with the galloper organ when Jack first had it, so he went down to Chiappas in London for some book music. He remembers delivering a 1948 Triumph 1800 Roadster sports car to someone in Weybridge in Surrey and then coming back to London and buying organ music with the money he had received for the Roadster.

Originally that organ, which dated from the 1870s, had no percussion, as was the case for all organs of that vintage. Showmen used to have a man with a big drum alongside their ride. This was cheaper than to have the organ altered. Then as time went on wings were added to the ends of organs to take percussion instruments. The main unit of Jack's one originally had a pinned barrel fitted and the hole where it went can still be seen in the back.

In its early life it was worked by a belt from an organ engine, which fitted on the steam centre engine of the gallopers, driving the barrel and working the bellows. Now Jack and Judith have had an electric blower fitted. At a fair you can draw the crowd with an electric blower so that you can start the music even if the steam is not quite up to pressure. Originally the organ was a 65-key one, but it has been converted down to 48-key.

### More sets of gallopers

About 1981, Jack bought galloper set No. 2. There were quite a few gallopers for sale at auction about that time. That one came up for sale at Cleethorpes, still before he was out travelling the Ashley set. Jack made contact with a Dr

Moorhead, headmistress of a girls school in Gloucestershire. She wanted a galloper for summer camp activities at the school. She came up to see that one at Cleethorpes, which was in the Wonderland amusement park and said that it would be suitable for her needs. Jack bid for it and bought it for her. He dismantled it, loaded it all up and took it down to the school, laid the site out, put the electricity in, put the concrete down, built it all up and got it all working. He earned enough for his time spent there to get the Ashley galloper nearly finished.

But that is not the end of that story. That set is now back in Jack's yard! When, much later, he and Judith went to the Fairford rally in Gloucestershire one August, Dr Moorhead came to see them and said she was going to retire and was looking for a good home for the gallopers. 'Would you like them, as you'd been such a help to me.' So Jack said 'Yes, but I'm afraid I haven't got any money. I've just bought a set of yachts. So she said 'What could I afford'. I said about £1500. 'That's all right' she said, 'You give me the £1500, we'll agree a price and you can pay it off over six years'.

So they fetched it in the October. So that's where his No.2 galloper came from. Jack says that it is complete, but a bit sort-of *tired*. It wants a lot of work done on it.

When it comes to Jack's No. 3 galloper, that came about like this. One year he and Judith were open at Anglesey rally and on the Friday night after they had built up, a showman came and sat on the platform and said, 'My family had one of these.' Jack was very interested and asked what happened to it. The showman said, 'We scrapped it.' which Jack thought was a shame. The conversation went on and then the showman said, 'But I might have some lampholders and other bits that could be useful to you.'

They went over to this showman's yard on the Monday – Mr Newsome was his name – and he found the lampholders and said, 'Take 'em, with pleasure, we don't use them any more, we use modern ones.' Then Jack said that it was a pity about the galloper being scrapped. 'Yes', he said, 'we've scrapped it. It's over there on the scrap heap.' Down at the bottom of the yard was this large heap of scrap about as high as a caravan and on the top was galvanised sheets, an old caravan chassis, barrels and tins and everything else. And down at the bottom was a galloper!

The showman had sold all the horses from the ride to Relic Design, the fairground antique dealers, and the rest was just scrap to him. The centre truck was cut up into three sections and the chimney was sliced in half, but all the gears were there, everything was there. The cranks hadn't been cut up and all the rods and the mechanics was there. So Jack did a deal on it and went over in the winter and dragged it out from all the other scrap. There was no timberwork at all, but there was all the metalwork – chimney, cheesewheel, cogs, cranks, bearings, everything to make a galloper! He has the full history and photos of that machine and it can be rebuilt and it would not be a *new* galloper but a rebuilt early machine from around the 1860s. It was originally Norths from Yorkshire, who sold it to Pickmere Lake Park in Cheshire. So that was how that one came to Jack Schofield.

The winter before that, Jack had been down to a sale at Burnham Beeches in Buckinghamshire and had bought a derelict galloper there. There is a whole tale with that one as well. It was sold *round the back* but the cranks were not with it and some other parts were missing. So Jack just bought the centre truck at the auction and then other parts including the cranks privately. It was stored in the corner of the Jack's yard and when he needed some money to get married he put it up for sale. That was the one that James Horton had.

**Steam Yachts**

Jack's set of steam yachts were delivered in May 1987. They were diesel driven when he got them. He and Judith looked a further four years before they could find a suitable steam engine for them. Originally the set had a vertical Robey engine. Everybody said to them, 'You'll not find one 'o them anywhere.' Jack was not deterred. He had heard one or two tales of where such things might be and a friend of his found one up on the Borders above Carlisle. Judith's mother lives near Penrith and so Jack sent Judith and her mum up to go and have a look. Off they went down a track and through a ford and eventually found the nursery, where there was a Robey portable engine. It was next to a bungalow and had been used for sterilising the green-house. This purchase enabled Jack to begin the ride restoration in earnest.

Jack sees his yachts as a loss-leader to help his gallopers but unfortunately just throwing money at them will not finish them. It takes time as well. 'You've just got to do the best you can in the winter months available. You're working to a deadline, to your going-out date. Whatever's not done by that date, isn't done! That's it for another year.' Most of the work that is left on the yachts is timberwork – staircases, landings, balustrading and front and back handrails. The two axles, which date from 1888 and are a vital part of the

*fig 40*
*Signwritten side of boat on Jack Schofield's steam yachts, awaiting completion of the ride. Painting by Kevin Scrivens*

ride, have been non-destructive tested and the 'boats' have been completely rebuilt.

'It's been a big job and it's still not finished. But I'm always hoping to finish it next year. But it depends on the season. You can only spend the money you've earned'

# John Carter & Family

No book about roundabout people would be complete without the inclusion of the Carter family. Their traditional steam fair, re-titled *Carters Royal Berkshire Steam Fair* in 1992 in support of the monarchy and perhaps to cock a snoot at the European Union, travels in Berkshire and neighbouring counties and in London. The family business is made up entirely of traditional old-time amusements, including two steam-powered rides – yachts and a set of gallopers. They particularly set out to appeal to the family market and travel five major rides in total, together with two sets of swingboats, a set of juvenile overboats dating from somewhere between 1875 and the early 1900s, juvenile car and train rides, a 'penny-in-the-slot' arcade and numerous hooplas and sidestalls. Their 1895 Tidman galloper is a central attraction. 'Don't ever call it a carousel,' says John, 'maybe a roundabout or a merry-go-round, but gallopers is the proper name for the English ride.'

The family are first-generation showfolk and are independents – not members of the Showmen's Guild. This means, among other things, that they are free to negotiate with local councils to appear with their fair at locations of their own choosing without the constraints of time and distance set by Guild rules. Town and village greens around London are favoured locations. John is a man of firm views, especially about how his fair is to be organised and presented to the public. The family success is in no small measure related to the funds they plough back into restoration and maintenance of equipment and into public relations and publicity. Supportive stories in the local press and national media are a regular feature of their travelling season, normally from late in March to late October. They open each weekend and on Bank Holiday Mondays.

John Carter's eclectic background includes going to the Slade School of Art, 'where I developed a *critical eye* but realised I would never be a great artist', and becoming a stock car racer to help with the fees. He has also been a bailiff, perhaps taking after his late father, who was a policeman and, with a foretaste of the future, a show promoter. His wife Anna is also art trained and she works during the winter months on fairground painting as well as carrying out her family roles. She is highly regarded as a scenic artist. There are three boys and two girls in their travelling family, Seth, Zed and Joby together with the girls Amber and Rose. Seth and his partner Tania presented the family with a grand-daughter Ashley at the end of 1995. All the family bring their various skills and their sheer muscle-power to the business. Joby has particular skills in the painting, scrolling and signwriting side, Amber, and Zed's partner Kathryn, show great abilities as coach painters and varnishers, all of which are essential skills in a business having so much painted equipment.

Recalling the quality of the 1964 Great Steam Fair at Shottesbrooke, John mentions that later attempts at repeating the event have never attained the atmosphere of the original. It

*fig 41*
*John & Anna Carter and family (left to right at back: Tania, young Ashley, Seth, Rosie, Anna & John, Kathryn and Zed, and in front, Joby and Amber Carter, plus the three dogs Buster, Moocher and Bully)*

was the first of its kind and will be remembered as such. Steam rallies nowadays fill their fairgrounds with a mix of a few traditional old-time rides and modern ones, thereby losing the unique atmosphere and spirit that was captured at Shottesbrooke. John himself attempted to match it with a promotion at Blackbushe in Hampshire in 1974, the tenth anniversary of John Smith's steam fair, which he judges was a reasonable success in spite of distractions from the nearby Blackbushe airport. There were eleven major old-time rides plus several fair organs and steam traction engines at this event.

Further books on various fun fair topics are now being produced at regular intervals, with the joint aims of recording and disseminating historical information and assisting with public relations. John is an avid collector of books, in spite of the difficulties of combining this with the travelling life. He is also a record collector of jazz, rhythm & blues and even rock & roll

*fig 42*
*Carters Steam Fair at Henley*

The Carter set of steam-powered gallopers reached their 100th year in 1995 and this was celebrated by the publication of a book about the ride written by pleasure fair historian Paul Braithwaite in conjunction with John Carter.

music and is keen on art deco. John and Anna's living van has an art deco interior. Anna herself is a collector of carnival glassware, so art and design remains very much part of their culture.

They are both frequent 'eaters out'. On one

*fig 43*
*Carters 1895 Tidman*
*gallopers*

memorable occasion at the time Anna was very pregnant with Rosie, they were about to go into a restaurant for a meal and their plans were interrupted by the slightly inconsiderate arrival of the baby. Anna says good-humouredly that all John could think about was missing his meal! He of course naturally denies having any such feelings.

### The Steam Gallopers

The ride was originally made in 1895 as far as can be ascertained, although no detailed records remain from the Tidman manufacturing business. It is thought that this particular machine was made for the Harris family from Sussex, who were related by marriage to the Matthews family, but the facts are not really known as to who traded the set with who in those early years. Since 1921 there have been six owners of the ride and in the 1950s it came to be installed at Burnham Beeches amusement grounds west of London. John Carter acquired it from there in late 1976. These rides have always been workhorses on the fairgrounds, in spite of waxing and waning in popularity at various times. The Carter set is believed to have opened to the public in every season since it was built.

The machine is 'English village' in size and style. It has the typical painted squares in red and cream on the platform steps, making it what is called a 'red set'. Seen also on Jack Schofield's gallopers, this decor is fairly unusual nowadays, as most other gallopers are based on cream and gold colouring. It is less elaborate and heavy than a fully-carved Savage set such as Noyce's. John Carter's machine today has 30 horses in the Anderson style, some of wood and some glass fibre, plus two chariots. It has a 46-key Gavioli organ dating from around 1900.

Recent changes to the ride in celebration of its centenary included adding a set of 26 double sided shields depicting English monarchs since 1066 and a new set of jungle scene paintings on the rounding boards. All of this painting work was done by Anna Carter, over two successive winters. The wooden rounding boards were refaced with thin aluminium sheet and ten different jungle scenes were painted on them. 'A bit of blood and gore this time' said Anna, perhaps reacting to the influence of recent television documentaries on African wildlife. If one looks carefully the viewer can detect the portrait of the Carters Rottwieler 'Buster' in one scene. Showfolk love to set little teases like this, just to see who detects them. Gold leaf to a value of £5000 was added to the rounding boards and top domes in that same winter of 1994/5. It was a race against time to get the work finished.

John says that the family still encounter objections and prejudices when they visit their

*fig 44*
*Galloper rounding*
*board jungle scene,*
*painted by Anna*
*Carter*

sites, especially where there has not been a fun-fair for many years. As John says, 'A crowd of seven thousand or more people enjoying themselves just has to be making a noise.' The family pay particular attention to any nearby inhabitants, giving out free ride tickets and copies of their latest book. In spite of trials and tribulations, the family continue with the unceasing work involved in running their fair and local councils continue to welcome their return in future years with their particular style of family amusements.

101

# James Graham

Now that he is 63 and semi-retired from the travelling business, Jimmy Graham says he is really enjoying himself. He reckons it does not take as much out of you if you are enjoying things. He owns a restored set of gallopers that was bought in 1984 from Wilmots, the original owners. These days the set appears mainly just at Holyrood Palace Park in Edinburgh at festival time in August and at the winter carnival from Christmas until mid-January in Glasgow.

Jimmy remembers so much of the old-time fairground equipment being just thrown away or burnt. He did not have the feel for it at the time but certainly regrets it now. He recalls buying an amusement arcade years ago and there were two old 'speak-your-weight' machines in it. As soon as he saw them it was 'Where's the pickup truck'. His son said 'For God's sake, dad, what are you going to do with all this rubbish'. In the back of one of these weighing machines there's just a record which simply plays at the place where their indicated weight has been recorded when someone stands on the machine.

Jimmy is on the Central Council of the Showmen's Guild and at the time of writing was their safety officer for Scotland. As such he has to set an example with his own equipment. For example with his chair ride he has the correct specified safety belts on each chair. 'I can't go to someone and say you've got to do this an' that if I don't toe the line myself.'

## Graham's Gallopers

The gallopers were only owned by a single family, the Wilmot's, before the Grahams bought them. They were built in 1885 as a swinging set without any platforms (a swingout lot). Like many other early sets, they were taken back to Savages to be converted into gallopers. One of the oldest sets of gallopers in the world, this machine has spent all its travelling life in Scotland. In its early years it was known as 'Wilmots Scottish National Steam Hippodrome' and after conversion to gallopers the name became 'Wilmot's Jubilee Galloping horses, the Safest and Most Sensational Riding Machine of the Day'. Perhaps what, at that time, might be viewed by riders as an advanced ride with jumping horses, led to this reassuring new name.

The first owner John Wilmot died in 1911 and his widow and sons continued to travel the ride and it was then given as a wedding present to Walter Wilmot. After the Second World War it was stripped of its elaborate carved work, making it easier to travel. When Grahams purchased them from Wilmot's grandson George Walter, the set was in very poor condition. The horses and the top centres from the ride had been sold to a dealer in London for about £3500. They were considered to be a lovely set of top centres with beautiful carved work round them. (Some of the historical information included above is from a description of UK Galloper G16, compiled by Kevin Scrivens and Stephen Smith).

The gallopers used to go to Newcastle Town Moor annual festival and when Wilmots next went there they had a Meteorite instead. The Northern Showmen's Syndicate, who are organisers of the Newcastle fair, would not let them put that on the ground. They said, 'No, that's a galloper position. You've got to fetch your gallopers or you're going to lose it.' So they had to go back to the man who had bought the horses and hire them back! It was said that it cost £1500, plus transporting them from London to Newcastle.

The original steam centre engine that was on the ride was sold for about fifteen pounds. Jimmy said that Wilmots had three organs in their yard in Glasgow and they just burnt them on a fire. As he says, 'If you think o' the stuff that was just thrown away and what it would be worth today.' All that was left of the original machine when Grahams bought it were the swifts, the quarterings and the Savage ironwork. Even the centres had to be replaced because the wood was all split. Leslie Burns, a showman who worked in Graham's yard, was a first class self-taught engineer and he lifted off the original top centre, laid it down as a pattern and just made another one.

Jimmy also extended the swifts about 18 inches because originally the rounding boards were in line with the outside row of horses. There was no protection for riders when it rained. Even now he still has things he wants to do. 'What I do want is another set of steps. Inside the Scottish exhibition centre where the ride is built up on the flat floor you don't notice it, but when you're out and you stand back the ride looks too low.'

*fig 45*
*James Graham*

made one mistake with these horses on the ride here now. Some designs have got an extra tail part on the back of the saddle and two people can get on comfortably and also it is easier to lift the animal when building up the ride. If you get two adults on mine it's just a bit tight.'

The complete ride was painted by Neddy Matthews, which involved Jimmy in several long trips south. But he thinks it was well worth it. The aim was to have something based on the designs and painting Neddy had done on Noyce's gallopers.

He would really like to have more of his gallopers restored in wood, rather than having to settle for glass fibre animals. 'Woody White carved twelve outside row horses for me, all in wood. I put them on the ride for special occasions. I'm in two minds whether to get another set of horses made for the next row. We only

The horse rods that Jimmy has are the large diameter type. He recalls once visiting a firm that made them and how the metal sections just went into a machine and came out twisted, 'So simple!' He really wants the ride to be bold.

*fig 46*
*James Graham's*
*gallopers at the*
*Winter Carnival in*
*Glasgow in December*
*1996*

Because when you look at it you can really see it there. The horses have the three inch size rods and the others are two inch. I try to make my gallopers a wee bit different, you know. I saw the oil lamps they used to have in some old books I've got of gallopers and I put in these white globes to look like them. They add another dimension to it. Everyone's got flags on their sets, so I thought I'd do something different. And I've a horse up over the top of the ride.'

fig 47
*Carved horse for
James Graham's
gallopers, carved by
Woody White &
painted by Neddy
Matthews. Sadie is
Jimmy Graham's
wife's name*

The names on the four cockerels and 32 horses are all Jimmy's father's grandchildren. At the time the animals were being painted there were 36 grandchildren. Jimmy comes from a big family himself with three boys and seven girls. As is often the way, his own children are not interested in gallopers – they will come and help if he is stuck but he thinks that if anything hap-

*fig 48*
*Carved horse with*
*Scottish flag and*
*whisky flask for James*
*Graham's gallopers,*
*carved by Woody*
*White and painted by*
*Neddy Matthews*

pens to him they will probably sell the lot. Jimmy's brother-in-law, Colin Sedgewick, who is also semi retired, helps him out.

Jimmy recalls a friend of his who has a Tidman set of gallopers. He was asking Jimmy all about gallopers when buying it. 'What he should do and that. I'll never forget one night last summer it was blowing a gale and he phoned me up. "Jimmy, it's blowing like hell here, what do I do?" I said, '*What do you mean, what do you do. You're a showman* (again that phrase which implies that showmen must always be self-sufficient). Just leave the blocks under it - don't try to open it.' He phoned me back the next night. "There was a few people about and I was dying to open it." But Jimmy replied, 'No, you can't do that. It's much too risky.'

Jimmy also remembers a trip to Turner's Musical Merry-go-Round at Northampton. 'He's got a set o' gallopers in there and I got talking to the owner when my wife and I went there. I said "What made you get into this?" Well, not knowing me, he was a wee bit wary…why do you want to know? I said "I am in this business. I'm a showman, a born and bred showman. I've a set of gallopers of my own, up in Scotland". He told me that he was fed up trying to get a place to put them up. People wanted more rent each year and didn't leave you enough of the takings to be worthwhile. They just seem to think you just go there, press a button and the ride takes all the money you want. They forget about all the costs, staff wages, maintenance and repair, fuel, insurance and so on.'

He recalls Jack Schofield who is restoring a set of steam yachts which were once owned by Jimmy's family. 'I served my time on them. I remember when it was steam driven.' Then his father had Jimmy Crow design a system using a diesel engine together with four back ends from lorries to drive them via wire ropes instead of steam. 'Marvellous! It was so simple.' That set used to be all wood, but Jimmy's father made two steel framed metal boats, which are what Jack has now.

Nowadays Jimmy Graham is just taking things steadily, travelling his gallopers just a few times each year. When he first settled down he missed being at all the major Scottish fairs, such as Kirkaldy Links and Bridge of Allan. But then he thinks about some of the 'hassles' of full-time travelling. Now he is just enjoying himself.

# The American Scene

The changing attitudes to merry-go-rounds in America are at least in part due to their own success. Many of the larger carousels were built as attractions for out-of-city parks, where transport companies operating the city trolley lines were keen to ensure their continued use at weekends and on holidays.

Carousel manufacturers were encouraged to employ the best skilled carvers, often immigrants from Germany, Italy and other European countries with established carving and wooden furniture making industries. These 'park machines' would normally be installed in their own permanent building.

When the popularity of such local amusement parks declined, as people became able to travel further afield and had other amusement distractions such as television, the value of carved animals on the rides as art pieces in their own right came to the fore. Menagerie animals such as lions, rabbits, cats, goats, giraffes and so on came to be seen as collectable fine art objects in contrast to their earlier naive art status (as they have largely remained in the UK). Prices fetched at present day auctions are often over $20,000, sometimes over $150,000 for a fine rare original well-restored carousel animal. Prices for English animals are usually well below one-tenth of these.

Owners of carousels were attracted by the financial gains of selling their rides at auction, normally broken down as individual pieces. The numbers of family and company owned operational carousels declined drastically and organisations such as the US National Carousel Association and the American Carousel Society were formed with the joint aims of preserving and restoring the remaining heritage, now numbering below 200 'antique' carousels.

One recent success was the purchase at auction of the complete carousel that used to operate at Euclid Beach in Cleveland. After all of the individual animals and mechanism had been bid, a further bid was forthcoming for the complete ride, at a world record price of $650,000, plus 10% buyers premium. This bid was placed by the US Trust for Public Land, probably nearest equivalent to the National Trust in the UK.

The interest in carved wooden animals as collectibles has also stimulated interest in the carving of new versions, both as collectable pieces and as replacements for use on carousels under restoration. The first carousel with a set of newly carved horses in the USA for over 60 years was created as a 'not-for-profit' undertaking in Missoula, Montana and opened to the public in 1995.

So who are 'Roundabout People' in the USA? They must surely include support groups – friends of the carousel – who, through voluntary efforts, have been able to ensure the preservation and reopening of many of the rides under threat. When a situation arises where an amusement park closes, often a support group with the aim of retaining the carousel is formed. Such a group becomes instrumental in lobbying and fund-raising, so that eventually the carousel is purchased by, for example, the closest city authority. The support group may often then become responsible for repaying a loan bond put up for the initial purchase and for providing skills for restoration and assistance with operation of the ride. The local 'Euclid Beach Park Nuts' is one such example.

Our 'roundabout people' should also include carvers and restorers, together with those leading members of enthusiast groups who encourage local support groups with skills, training and funding help. This participative environment leads to substantial involvement of volunteers from people with more disposable income than is normal in enthusiast groups in the UK, such as teachers, local government workers and others.

But there are exceptions to the decline in the fortunes of the amusement park industry. Those parks that were able to make major investments in new rides, particularly roller-coasters, and who were also able to promote themselves as holiday attractions or major themed parks, are still with us today. Then there are purpose-built post-war theme parks, the major examples being the various Disney ventures, where there remain some fine examples of historic carousels still in operation.

*fig 49*
*Trimper's Herschell-Spillman carousel at Ocean City, Maryland. This ride was purchased new and installed at the Trimper's park in 1902*

## Trimpers

Trimpers Amusement Park in Ocean City, Maryland was established in 1893 and is still run by the same family. At least eight of the family in three generations work today at their seaside park. Granville Trimper took over full management of the park in 1980. Today they have over 100 rides, most of which are installed in the open air, but they take pride in still operating a selection of old-time Mangels rides dating from the 1920s and their 1902 Herschell-Spillman carousel. The Mangels rides were bought in the boom immediately after the First World War and include a kiddie carousel, a kiddie whip, dodgems (called bumper cars in the US) a kiddie ferris wheel and a sea-on-land boat ride.

The carousel has been owned by the Trimper family and installed at the same location since it was new. It was initially powered by steam but has been converted to electric drive.

Made by Herschell-Spillman of North Tonawanda, New York State, it has a total of 55 animals. The outer of the three rows are standers, there are four chariots and a rocking coach, whilst the middle and inner row animals are jumpers (gallopers as we would say in the UK).

The menagerie comprises a lion, a sea dragon, a camel, a tiger, a deer, two each of ostriches, giraffes, cockerels, cats, frogs, dogs, pigs and donkeys, with the rest being horses. A total restoration of the animals was undertaken in 1980. Each one was stripped back coat by coat to discover the original colours and decoration. All broken parts were restored with new carved replacements. John and Maria Bilous took three years to complete this work.

Music from a replica Wurlitzer band

*fig 50*
*Herschell-Spillman*
*standing tiger on*
*Trimper's carousel*

organ installed close by accompanies the ride. The carousel is a favourite with the four young grandchildren – Chelsea, Matt, Adam and Timothy. Granville Trimper sees it as a family heirloom.

## All Hallows Guild Carousel

In contrast to the more elaborate Trimpers carousel, this simple early machine

*fig 51*
*US Merry-Go-Round*
*1890s portable*
*carousel at*
*Washington Cathedral*
*All Hallows Guild,*
*September 1996*

was made by the US Merry-Go-Round Company of Cincinnati in the 1890s. It is believed to be the last one made by that company. The light carving style is much more 'naive folk art' than that seen on Trimpers machine. It is a two row machine and was made to be easily portable. These simpler constructions came to be called the County Fair Style. The carousels were made lighter than permanent park machines to be more suitable for travelling.

This carousel was purchased by members of the All Hallows Guild of Washington Cathedral DC in 1963 and is only built up and operated at their May Flower Mart fund-raising event and for one day in September. The carousel is built up in the Cathedral grounds with extensive views over the city of Washington. There are 22 animals on the ride, a lion, an elephant, a zebra, two goats, two reindeer, two camels and thirteen horses. plus two chariots. Music comes from a rare brass-piped Caliola made by the Wurlitzer Company, dated to the late 1920s/early 1930s, which plays piano-style music rolls.

Restoration work is carried out by members of the All Hallows Guild and by members of the National Society of Decorative Painters. A number of donors have underwritten the costs of the restoration of each animal as a memorial.

### Riverfront Park Carousel, Spokane

In eastern Washington State there is a magnificent Looff carousel owned by the City of Spokane and operated in a purpose built pavilion in the city centre Riverside Park. Charles Looff built Coney Island's first carousel in 1876 and was asked to visit Natatorium Park in Spokane in 1907 where, naturally, he recommended that the park install a carousel. This was completed and opened at the park in 1909. The 'Nat' as it was known, was a popular picnic location which developed over the years with swimming, concert and baseball facilities as well as amusement rides. It was a favourite with US servicemen during World War Two, but like many others, went through hard times in the 1960s. The park closed in 1968 and the carousel went into storage.

The carousel was purchased by the City authorities after a local fund-raising campaign and, after restoration, opened on its present site in 1975. It is a three row park carousel with 54 jumping horses, a tiger, a giraffe and two dragon chariots. It is one of the few remaining carousels with an operating ring machine, which enables skilled outside row riders to 'grab the brass ring', entitling them to a reward, usually a free ride. The rings are plastic rather than brass nowadays for cost reasons. Each of the horses is differently carved in its details, Looff doing much of the carving himself. The ride still has its original mechanical gearing and 15 hp electric drive motor.

Maintenance and restoration work today is in the hands of a team of trained volunteers. Tuition sessions are regularly held at Riverside Park to instruct others in the arts and crafts involved.

The organ for the ride was made by Ruth of Waldkirch, Germany in 1907 and had a major overhaul by the BAB Company of Brooklyn in the 1940s, when it was also converted to play

*fig 52*
*1909 Looff carousel at*
*Riverfront Park,*
*Spokane, Washington*
*State, October 1995*

using the paper roll system instead of book music. It is now rather fragile and is played only occasionally, with band organ recordings being used at other times.

**Burnaby Carousel, British Columbia**

In the built-up area around Vancouver there is another prime example of an antique American carousel saved by local public initiative.

115

This is a C.W.Parker machine built in 1912. It is installed at Burnaby Village Museum, a reconstructed village representing a typical tram-stop community in British Columbia in the years around 1900-25. The village comprises over thirty reconstructed buildings, including shops, homes, a church, and a schoolhouse. One of its main roles is children's education.

This Parker carousel operated in Texas and in California in its early years. From around 1934 to 1989 it was successively at two parks in the Vancouver area. Happyland, the first of these, closed in 1957 and the carousel was moved to a new park called Playland.

One of the local girls that rode the carousel in the 1960s was Venus Solano. Later, she worked as a waitress at the park and in the winter of 1986/7 she was involved in attempts to refurbish the machine which was at that time in poor condition. She heard of the proposed auctioning of the carousel and intent to sell off the horses individually, a situation that has been and often still is the fate of these valuable antique wooden machines.

Venus Solano led a major campaign to raise awareness of this impending loss, with media attention and the assistance of Fred Fried, who was a leading figure in the carousel preservation movement. To cut a long story short, eventually a group of 'Friends of the Carousel' was formed, monies and pledges were raised by public appeals, a bond was forthcoming from the city authorities and a team of trained volunteers set about restoring the machine and the animals. The purchase price involved was $330,000 dollars plus sales tax.

The volunteer teams set to work over the period 1990 to 1993. A new pavilion to house the ride was built at Burnaby Village, the Don Wrigley pavilion, named after the president of the Friends group. After many trials and tribulations, the fully restored C.W.Parker Carousel, number 119, was opened to the public. The 'Roundabout People' had triumphed. Members of this team were subsequently involved in the restoration of the Jantzen Beach antique carousel now installed in a shopping mall in Portland, Oregon.

**Reconstruction of the Eden Palais Salon Carousel**

Built in the late 1800s, Salon Carousels might be called the 'entertainment centres' of

*fig 53*
*Stargazer horse*
*restored by Friends of*
*the Carousel on*
*C.W.Parker carousel*
*at Burnaby BC,*
*Canada*

their time. They were hugely ornate structures with elaborate showfronts and complete enclosures separating visitors from the general bustle of the surrounding scene. Inside there would be various bars and other live entertainment in addition to the centrepiece carousel and its accompanying organ. They were popular in mainland Europe rather than in the UK. Only five are thought to still exist, one being at Efterling Park in The Nederlands, illustrated in *Fairground Art*.

*fig 54*
*Facade of the Eden*
*Palais salon carousel,*
*under restoration in*
*August 1997 at*
*Sanfilippo's estate.*

The one known as the 'Eden Palais' salon carousel was exported to the USA in the 1950s. It was never fully assembled and at one stage came to be stored in the open under snow! By the late 1980s was in a very dilapidated condition. Tim Trager, an American acquaintance of Stephen & Vicky Posthethwaite mentioned its existence to them when he was in England. It was purchased by Marian & Jasper Sanfilippo of Barrington Hills, Illinois in 1987 and has

*fig 55*
*Gavioli organ front*
*and top centre of the*
*Eden Palais salon*
*carousel, August 1997*

been under restoration for ten years, with an estimated further year of work required to completion. It first operated as part of the Sanfilippo collection on 30th July 1997. This virtually unique ride has been lovingly – and very expensively – restored and the illustrations here show the stage of this work as in mid-August 1997.

Carousels of this size and content required the combined skills of several manufacturers when first they were made. This one was com-

119

*fig 56*
*German Hubner*
*horses and lover's tub*
*under restoration on*
*the Eden Palais salon*
*carousel, August 1997*

pleted c1890, with the facade by Devos of Belgium, carousel horses by Hübner of Germany, mechanism by Köning, gondolas and centre by Moulinas of Belgium, paintings by Coppier of France and a Gavioli organ. Restoration has called for a similar wide range of differing skills, over 20 dedicated individuals and companies being involved, including Will Morton,

Rosa Ragan, Tony D'Angelo, Carousel Works staff, and Johnny Verbeeck on rebuild of the 89-key Gavioli organ in Belgium.

The salon carousel was originally owned and travelled in north-west Europe by the Bruckman family and later by the Demeyer family. In 1927 the owners were the Caron Brothers and they remodelled it and travelled it in Europe under the 'Eden Palais' name. When it was exported to the USA in about 1959, it had two owners before the Sanfilippos.

Reconstruction and presentation of the complete ride is in a new purpose built carousel building on the Sanfilippo estate. The facade is of baroque and art nouveau styling and measures 93 feet in width and 38 feet in height. An elaborate art nouveau paybox stands in the centre doorways of the facade and visitors enter to see the centre truck mounted carousel. This is driven by an under platform mechanism. The ornate top centre of the ride rotates in the reverse direction to the anti-clockwise motion of the platform. There is a rocking lovers tub, a chariot and 36 rocking horses on the ride.

It is likely that followers of the history of travelling fairs/carnivals will see it as a supreme example of re-creation of the ultimate from the heyday of the turn of the 19th century. It represents much more than the phrase 'roundabout people' can convey and is a fitting finale to the American Scene chapter.

EPILOGUE

# Epilogue

## Jimmy Williams

*Jimmy Williams is a retired showman and fair-ground painter. He has travelled gallopers for over 25 years and still takes great pride in the set that he has kept since he stopped travelling. His remarks touch on many of the topics covered in earlier chapters and make a fitting finale.*

'We used to go to Newbury Show, to Knowle Hill, to Woodcote. The first season I went out, I did 32 rallies, one week after another. We did all our own places, I never went in with anyone else. I travelled about 24 years on my own account. The business was all right, I loved the business. The only trouble was getting the right labour. The rally secretaries were like friends in those days. The engine men used to come over and you'd all sit round a fire in the evening time and have a chat with them and they'd have a chat with you.

That set of gallopers that are in America now were the first ones as ever I bought. We travelled with that for four or five years, then it had to go for death duties. That machine belonged to Beeches. It was a very nice light machine. Then my parents both died and in those days there were death duties to pay and that machine had to go. I sold it, through an agent, to Warner Brothers, the park owners.

From recent photos, it looks as if they've painted the horses since I last saw it. But the cockerels look about the same as when they went over, I think. The outside row horses are Andersons and the inside row are Savages, carved nicely, but with straight legs in the front. The cockerels are the same as I have on my machine here now – Orton & Spooners.

Then I bought the switchback. I travelled that for one season. But it was too heavy. You can't really live in the past, not too much. We were trying to travel that with just two men, whereas in its heyday they had an army of men. I bought it off Manning at Southsea. Believe you me, I did 22 places with it in that one season. That was a monster of a thing! My weight got down to 11

*fig 57
Teddy Reed's
Hooghuys organ front,
restored by Jimmy
Williams*

stone, travelling that! It was too heavy and it never rode full. The day of the switchback ended in the 1920s. The scenics and the switchbacks had very short lives. The rides ruined a lot of showmen because they had to use them right up to the last wartime, to pay back the instalments owing on them. It kept them poor. Then

season, then I got a carver to carve new rounding boards, swifts and so on. We spent a lot of time on that machine. It's very strong. I've seen 20 or 30 people jump on one side and it just wouldn't move! You see, it was a four abreast at the start, and then it was cut down to a three abreast. The middle was built strong to take the weight

the same people from America got hold of me and said they'd like it in the park over there. My wife Bunch was never so pleased to see a machine go in her life.

So that went, and I bought the roundabout that I've got now, from Whiteleggs. It was at Exeter and it had been stored for about 15 years. I got it home and had carpenters make a new platform and steps. We travelled it as it was for one

of a four abreast. It's got a seven foot six centre drum, compared to the ordinary standard one of about four foot six. All the animals are wood. I believe that on a *true* machine they must be authentic and not fibreglass copies.

My father was a fair painter. I copied a lot of the showman's type of painting off of him. The biggest restoring job I ever did was the two organs that were damaged by the fire at Teddy

Reed's. The Gavioli was badly damaged but was restored just like it was originally. I think the last man to do it was Tiller, who used to work for Chiappas. There's a terrific amount of gold leaf

three or four years ago they took the old canvas off and traced exactly the same design as I did onto the front that is there now. I painted the front of the wheel there and the rounding boards on the

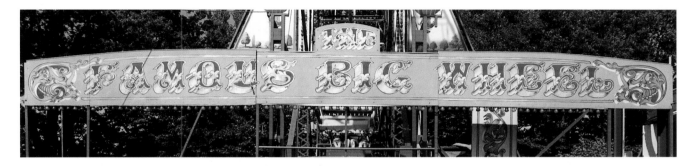

*fig 58*
*Big Wheel showfront*
*at Hollycombe*
*painted and gilded by*
*Jimmy Williams*

I've put on it. And there's a lot of silver as well. I've done it exactly the same as it was by Tiller.

When it came to the Hooghuys, Teddy said it was never painted properly in the first place, so I could do it more in my own style. I've also been doing a lot of figures in Teddy's collection. I've put a terrific amount of gold on them. Flamboyant paint is all right, but I think it's a bit commercial, a bit cheapjack. Gold is the thing, because if it's looked after, it will last a lifetime.

I used to do a lot of painting for Commander Baldock at Hollycombe. I did the bioscope show, the top, on canvas, because that's how it used to be. He used it for 15 or 18 years like that. About

razzle-dazzle. I did that single steam yacht when he first had it and it went to White Waltham Steam Fair.

I've painted a lot of Romany caravans. The first one, about 35 or 40 years ago, was for the Fleet caravan company. It was a Reading-style wagon and was in their showroom for years. I've done 18 or 20 of those wagons. I did one for a Pearly King man from Enfield. He was in that picture *Dr Doolittle* with it.

The last time I took my galloper set out was to Newbury Show. We did Newbury Show for donkey's years, from when my father was alive. I took gallopers there myself for 22 years until the last time, about 7 or 8 years ago. Then I sold my dodgems to Heals, at Brighton and the twist that I had to Burnetts.

But I retained the gallopers, I wouldn't sell them. I've done a lot of work on them and I'd hate anybody to have them that would mistreat them. It would be different if it was to go to a museum or something like that where it would be looked after.

I haven't been too well and the doctors advised me not to do any painting for six months. So I said we'll get that centre truck out instead and rebuild it. What we found was that when Savages first made it in 1896, it was a low centre truck, for going by rail, and the actual truck was wooden framed, great big 4x4 inch timbers. We replaced the wood frame with iron, to the same design as that Savages used around 1900. I'm amusing myself now putting all the wooden bits on. I've been doing that for a couple of months, but when I was a bit younger, I'd have done it in a fortnight.

Really, it's a job to keep off the painting. I enjoy painting better than I do travelling. It's a funny thing, because we were bred and born showmen, my father and my grandfather, going back about seven generations. With travelling there's a lot of headaches. It's nice when it's nice, but there's a lot of worries in between.'

*Although stored for the last few years, Jimmy Williams gallopers remain his pride and joy. They are kept in immaculate condition, together with the Gaudin organ from the ride. He says that he would really like to leave the set to a working museum, who would look after the ride properly. Galloper men all – Jimmy and all the others whose stories you have heard.*

# Cavalcade

## Gallopers in operation

Ayers

Beardow

Lythgoe (ex-Dorman)

Downs

Forrest

Hollycombe Collection

Mason (Meech)

Noyce

Pettigrove

Rawlins

Rule

Screeton/Armitage

*fig 59*
*An example of the*
*horses on Ayers*
*gallopers. Painted by*
*Bobby Ayers*

Ayers gallopers were built by Savages in 1893 and sold to William Beach, later being operated by his daughter Sally. In 1975 they passed to her niece Eileen Ayers and her husband Frank.

They are now operated by Bertie and Tommy Ayers. The 36 horses are all Wooden 'Colonial' style and were recently painted by Bobby Ayers. The organ is an 89 key Gavioli (see p.78)

*fig 60*
*Ayers gallopers at the*
*Bath & West Show,*
*Shepton Mallet,*
*Somerset, 1997*

*fig 61*
*Finely carved Savage*
*Victory horse on*
*Beardow's gallopers*

The centre board on this set of Savage gallopers gives 1918 as their date, although they were actually delivered in 1920. They were initially owned by George Tuby and subsequently by Tom Drakeley in the West Midlands. The set is currently (in 1997) owned by Raymond Beardow and is at Brean Leisure Park in Somerset. It has a magnificent set of carved rounding board droppers and heavily carved 'Victory Horses' from Savage and Orton & Spooner workshops.

*fig 62*
*Beardow's gallopers*
*at Brean Leisure Park,*
*Somerset, September*
*1997*

*fig 63*
*Dorman's galloper*
*horse and centre*
*shutters, the latter*
*painted by Jimmy*
*Williams*

Widely known as the Dorman's no.1 set, this machine is now owned by Frank Lythgoe of Lymm, Cheshire, who purchased it in 1994. It was built by Savages as a 'dobby' set in 1882 and was initially horse-drawn. It is a 14-section machine with two chariots, six cockerels and 30 horses, now in glass fibre. It is steam powered and fitted with Savage centre engine no.903. The elaborately carved bottom centre panels were restored by Jimmy Williams. It has an 89 key Gavioli organ.

*fig 64*
*Dorman's gallopers at*
*Pickering Steam*
*Rally, 1997*

*fig 65*
*Outside row horse on*
*David Downs*
*gallopers, painted by*
*Johnny Hatwell*

Downs gallopers have been made up from two earlier sets of Tidman gallopers, one dating from the 1890s. Allan Downs acquired one set in the 1940s and the second, in derelict condition, in the early 1950s. They are now owned and operated by his grandson David Downs. They have a Savage steam centre engine fitted, which is used in place of electric power on special occasions. The horses are now all glass fibre, most recently decorated by Johnny Hatwell. There is an 89 key Gavioli organ on the machine.

*fig 66*
*Downs gallopers at*
*the Great Dorset*
*Steam Fair, 1996, with*
*David's mother Vylma*
*Downs on the*
*platform*

*fig 67*
*Three-abreast row of*
*ostriches on Forrest's*
*gallopers*

This ride is thought to have been made by Howcroft's in about 1890. It has been in the Forrest family since 1921. A major feature is the rare menagerie of six bears, six ostriches and six chickens carved by Andersons, together with 18 horses carved by Orton & Spooners. It has a 65 key Gavioli organ. The rounding boards carry lettering by Lakin's craftsmen and the platform steps have been marbled by Vicky Postlethwaite, who has also redecorated the organ front. The horses have been repainted by James Horton. It is an excellent example of a traditional ride.

*fig 68*
*Forrest's gallopers at*
*the Great Dorset*
*Steam Fair, August*
*1997*

*fig 69*
*Rounding boards on*
*the gallopers at*
*Hollycombe,*
*decorated by Fred*
*Fowle*

The Hollycombe Steam Collection gallopers were built by Tidmans in about 1912. This machine was acquired for the Hollycombe Collection in 1986. A Tidman centre engine of early 1900s vintage has been fitted and allows the set to be steam powered. There are 24 horses, six cockerels and two chariots. The decor is by Fred Fowle. It is fitted with a 46 keyless Leach organ.

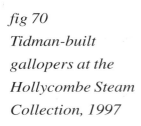

*fig 70*
*Tidman-built*
*gallopers at the*
*Hollycombe Steam*
*Collection, 1997*

*fig 71*
*Chariot on Mason's*
*gallopers, painted by*
*Lee Meech, winter*
*1996/7*

*fig 72*
*Mason's gallopers at*
*Goring-on-Thames*
*regatta, 1997*

Masons gallopers are thought to have been built by Walkers around the turn of the 19th century. After travelling into the 1970s, the ride eventually was owned by the Noble Organisation and installed on the Palace Pier at Brighton. Jimmy Meech, who travels as 'Masons Amusements', bought the ride in 1991. It has been extensively renovated and in 1996/7 the centres, paybox and chariots were repainted by his son Lee Meech. It has a 48 key Page and Howard organ.

*fig 73*
*Carved centres on*
*Noyce's gallopers*

This very well-known set is travelled by Jimmy and Tommy Noyce. It was Savage-built in the 1890s for Studt's. It was upgraded and fitted with J.R.Anderson carved replacement horses in 1900-1. It has six cockerels and 30 horses. The rounding boards and the centres have particularly elaborate carving. It has an 89 key Gavioli organ.

*fig 74*
*Noyce's gallopers in*
*Leicester Square,*
*London at Christmas*
*1992*

*fig 75*
*Hanging dragon*
*chariot on*
*Pettigrove's gallopers*

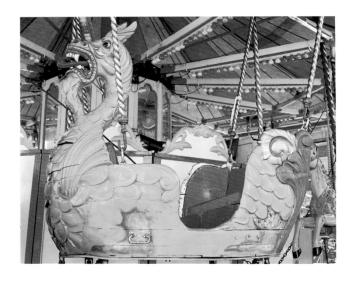

*fig 76*
*Pettigrove's gallopers*
*at Thame Show fair,*
*1997*

This set was built by Tidmans in about 1881 as a dobby set and later upgraded to gallopers. It has been owned by the Pettigrove family since new. The centre row horses are glass fibre but the others are wood, some being signed by Orton & Spooner. There are two unusual hanging dragon chariots on the ride. These were obtained from the British Empire exhibition of 1924. The rounding boards were newly signwritten in 1997.

*fig 77*
*Horse with decorated*
*step on Rawlins*
*gallopers. The*
*platform decor by*
*Mark Gill is*
*particularly attractive*

This is an 1893-built Savage set which was later travelled by the Matthews family from the 1920s. In 1946 it was owned by John Beach and '*Pride of the South*' lettering was placed on the rounding boards. It passed to son-in-law Bobby Rawlins in 1976. This largely original set has featured in many films. The 36 horses are all wood. Extensive redecoration has been undertaken by Mark Gill, particularly on the steps and rounding boards. It is now complemented by a Gaudin organ.

*fig 78*
*Bobby Rawlins*
*gallopers at Knowle*
*Hill Rally, Berkshire,*
*1997*

*fig 79*
*Gavioli organ on*
*Rule's gallopers*

*fig 80*
*Rule's gallopers at*
*their first appearance*
*at the Tallington* Old
Glory *rally in 1993*

Rule's gallopers were the subject of a major rebuild over a period of nine years, coming out under their ownership in 1993 at the first *Old Glory* Tallington rally. They originally started life as a Savage machine built in the mid 1890s. The ride spent many years at Collins parks in Seaburn and Barry Island. It now has a Tidman steam centre engine and a Gavioli organ.

*fig 81*
*Signwork on transport*
*in front of Armitage's*
*Screeton's gallopers*

*fig 82*
*Screeton's gallopers*
*at Boston May Fair*
*1997*

This set is now travelled by John Armitage and his wife Rosalie, née Screeton. It possibly started life as an Allen built 'dobby' set and was upgraded to a galloper by Savages in the 1890s. When it was sold to the Screeton Brothers in 1966, all the horses had been replaced by glass fibre versions. It has been refitted with a steam centre engine and this is used instead of electric drive at special events. The ride is under active redecoration. It has an 89 key Gavioli organ.

BIBLIOGRAPHY

# Bibliography

## Books and catalogues

*The Travelling People*, Duncan Dallas, Macmillan, 1971. SBN 333 002970.

*The Fairground*, Ian Starsmore, Whitechapel Gallery exhibition catalogue, 1977

*Fairground Art*, Weedon and Ward, New Cavendish, 1981. ISBN 0 904568 28 8.

*Painted Ponies-American Carousel Art*, Manns, Shank and Stevens, Zon International, 1986. ISBN 0 939549 01 8.

*Grab the Brass Ring*, Anne Hinds, Random House (Crown Publishers), 1990. ISBN 0 517 57486 1.

*Fairfield Folk*, Frances Brown, Ronda Books, 1993. ISBN 0 9521282 0 9

*Traditional English Gallopers*, booklet by Paul Braithwaite, 1994.

*People's Art*, Emmanuel Cooper, Mainstream Publishing, 1994. ISBN 1 85158 108 1.

*Jump On, Jump On*, Brian Steptoe, Navigator Books, 1994. ISBN 0 902830 33 3.

*Jubilee Steam Gallopers*, Paul Braithwaite, Carter Books, 1995.

*A Carousel is Magic*, Annie Boulanger, Friends of the Vancouver Carousel, 1995. ISBN 0 9699929 0 4.

*Tussauds collection of Fairground Art*, Christie's auction sale catalogue, 1997.

*Gallopers*, S.Smith and K.Scrivens, Fairground Association of Great Britain, 1998. ISBN 0 9513835 4 X

## Video

The Great Steam Fair, video version of Cinemascope film of the 1964 Shottesbrook Steam Fair

## Internet sites

www.carousel.org, Carousel home page

www.carousel.org/gallopers.html, UK Galloper news reports

www.shef.ac.uk/~nfa, University of Sheffield: National Fairground Archive

www.ndirect.co.uk/~fops, Fair Organ Preservation Society

www.rgs.u-net.com/, Hollycombe Steam Collection

(internet website addresses are correct at the time of writing but are subject to change)

# Illustrations

page            page

# Index